"Rob Rienow has done an incredible job of capturing the burden that so many parents feel for their adult children. He provides practical and God-honoring advice to bring the hearts of your children back to God. *When They Turn Away* brings you hope even in the midst of painful times. I will pass this book to anyone who is bewildered by the fact that their children are not following after their faith."

—**Jim Burns**, President, HomeWord, Author of *Confident Parenting*

"In this hope-filled book, Rob captures the underlying pain of empty nesters; the pain of a wayward child. Each chapter is a personal and practical journey of what to do and what not to do to manifest the character of Christ to your son or daughter. This book is all about HOPE! Parents need a strategy, they need well crafted words to balance grace and truth, and they need to know God expects them to pursue and move toward their lost child. Without a doubt, this book will recover a lost generation!"

—**Pastor Ron Brenning**, Grace Chapel, Englewood, CO

"Rob Rienow has done a fantastic job tackling a subject that millions of mid-life and older Christians are facing. This book empowers parents to win back the hearts of their adult children and ultimately lead them to Christ. Every Christian parent who longs to see their adult child walk with Christ should read this book and put the principles into practice."

—**Dr. Amy Hanson**, speaker, consultant, adult ministry specialist and author of *Baby Boomers and Beyond: Tapping the Ministry Talents and Passions of Adults over 50*

"Rienow shares from personal experience, years of pastoral ministry, and a passion for the home and grace-shaped people in this book for parents. Parents: read this book. If not for yourself . . . you know some friends who are experiencing this very thing and need this book. Saturated with the Word, this book will encourage you in the intense battle for your child's soul."

—**Kim Davidson**, Family Discipleship Director, Providence Baptist Church

"Rob Rienow writes to all parents or grandparents that grieve over paths their adult children have taken. *When They Turn Away* tells "what happened" while we were safely cloistered at church and poses the question, is it too late for us to counter a secular culture's spiritual sway on our adult children? Rob says no, and pulls back the curtain on the lie that we no longer have influence in their lives."

—**Ward Tannenberg**, Executive Director, CASA Network

"[*When They Turn Away*] is practical, biblical, simple, relevant."

—**Dr. Scott Turansky**, National Center for Biblical Parenting

WHEN THEY TURN AWAY

DRAWING YOUR ADULT CHILD
BACK *to* CHRIST

Rob Rienow

Kregel
Publications

When They Turn Away: Drawing Your Adult Child Back to Christ

© 2011 by Rob Rienow

Published by Kregel Publications, a division of Kregel, Inc., 2450 Oak Industrial Dr. NE, Grand Rapids, MI 49505.

Scripture taken from the HOLY BIBLE, NEW INTER-NATIONAL VERSION®. NIV®. Copyright © 1973, 1978, 1984 by International Bible Society. Used by permission of Zondervan. All rights reserved.

Scripture quotations marked NKJV are from the New King James Version. Copyright © 1982 by Thomas Nelson, Inc. Used by permission. All rights reserved.

The persons and events portrayed in this book have been used with permission. To protect the privacy of these individuals, some names and identifying details have been changed.

ISBN 978-0-8254-3653-6

Printed in the United States of America
15 16 17 18 19 20 21 22 23 24 / 7 6 5 4 3

To my father,

Bill Rienow,

who taught me that

it is never too late

to turn to God.

I am eager to

see you in heaven.

CONTENTS

PREFACE

"I HAVE NO GREATER joy than to hear that my children are walking in the truth" (3 John 4).

You are reading this book because you know that the opposite is also true. There is no greater sorrow for Christian parents than to know our children are not faithfully following Christ.

We desperately want our children to have deep faith and a personal relationship with God through Jesus Christ. We want our families to have warm, close fellowship together throughout our lives. Most of all, we want to arrive safely home in heaven together with our children.

For many parents these seem like dreams that need to be abandoned. But there is hope, because God is still on His throne.

Before we begin, though, I need to address an elephant in the room. I do not have adult children yet. Amy and I have been blessed with six children ranging in age from one to thirteen years. So what am I doing writing a book about parenting adult children?

There are two reasons. First, I spent a decade of my pastoral life as a youth minister, working specifically with high school students and their families. I led a large youth ministry that had more than 350 active students involved each year. God did wonderful things in the lives of these young people. I'm thankful that my relationships with many of these students did not end after they left high school. I've lost track of the number of weddings I've performed for students who grew up in the youth group, and now many of them have children of their own.

It gives me great sorrow, however, that the majority of the students who seemed to be on track spiritually as juniors and seniors in high school are now no longer walking with the Lord. I used to believe that if a young person was following God faithfully at age eighteen, the spiritual cement had hardened and they were on track to follow God for a lifetime. I no longer believe that.

Show me young men and women following God at age twenty-five, however, and we find a much clearer picture as to how true and deep their faith is. So it naturally followed that ministering to high school students progressed into ministry for "twenty-somethings." I was then in the position of trying to encourage faith in young adults who had grown up in the church, but who were in the far country, like the prodigal son. I was also deeply engaged with the parents of these young adults, and they were brokenhearted that their children had turned away from God and from the church.

My second reason for this book is that, a few years ago, God led Amy and me to begin a ministry called Visionary Parenting. It was birthed out of a time of deep repentance and brokenness, as I needed to confess that I was not putting my wife and children first in my life. I was not the spiritual leader of my home, and was doing nothing in an intentional way to pass on my faith to my own children. But the Lord changed my heart, my life, and our family.

When I began making presentations to parents at Visionary Parenting conferences, a clear pattern emerged. After I finished speaking, time after time, men and women would come up to me saying something like, "Rob, we really appreciated what you said… but our daughter is twenty-four. All the things you talked about apply to parents with children still in the home," or "Our child is an adult… and he's far from God." These parents often asked through tears, "What do we do now?"

This cry was coming from all directions. God was filling my life not only with young adults who were struggling with faith, but with their parents as well. I knew my personal opinions weren't going to offer the right direction, and pat answers were useless. The Lord made it clear to me that I needed to search the Scriptures so I could answer the question, "What do we do now?"

My prayer is that God will use the words of this book to point you to the words in His Book. He has not left us alone to figure out for ourselves how to help our wayward children. God has given parents specific guidance and direction so that we might encourage faith in the hearts of our children—no matter how old they are.

ACKNOWLEDGMENTS

I GIVE ALL THANKS to God who has forgiven my sin and saved me through the death and resurrection of Jesus Christ. Next to salvation, the greatest gift God has given to me is my wife, Amy, and our six children. Amy, you have helped me in every way toward becoming the man God wants me to be.

Thanks to my mother, who raised me to know the Lord and love Him, and to my stepfather, Jack, who loves God and my mom. Both of you have put in countless hours of editorial work to make this book possible.

I'm grateful for the members of the Epaphrodites Adult Class at Wheaton Bible Church who encouraged me to pursue this project. Many of you know how much it hurts to have grown children far from God. Thank you for sharing your hearts and stories with me.

Thanks to all those who gave permission for me to share their stories in the pages ahead. Your names have been changed to protect your identity.

The Kregel team has been terrific. You've helped make the ministry of this book stronger every step of the way.

Last but not least, I'm grateful for my father, who is home in heaven with Jesus. He taught me that it's never too late to turn to God.

Chapter 1

HOW COULD THIS HAPPEN?

I FIRST MET MIKE when he was a high school student. He participated in our youth group's annual hiking trip on the Appalachian Trail. When you're hiking, there isn't much to do besides talk, and God provided me with an opportunity to share with him the message of the gospel. By God's grace, in the middle of the wilderness, Mike responded and put his faith and trust in Jesus. He came back and became very involved in the life of our church. He rose to be a leader in the youth group and after graduating came back and worked to mentor the younger students. I longed to see more young men like this one.

Fast-forward eight years. Mike had moved away to another part of the country. I was in my office and the phone rang. "Hi, Rob! It's Mike. Do you remember me? I'm engaged, am moving back to the area, and would like you to do our premarital counseling." I was thrilled to hear the news, and immediately arranged a time to reconnect with Mike and meet his fiancée.

Within the first few minutes of our meeting, it became apparent to me that Mike's fiancée was not a Christian. I began to gently probe into that issue by sharing with them how unity is at the core of a healthy marriage—two people becoming one—and I sensed that they might be in different places when it came to matters of faith and spirituality. It was an awkward but necessary conversation. My gentle approach didn't seem to be working, so I turned up the volume and asked, "What happens if God blesses you with children? What would be your plan for their spiritual training?" At this point, Mike looked at me and said, "I guess we're going to let our kids figure that stuff out on their own. There are a lot of different ways to God. I don't think Jesus is the only way, and I don't think that the Bible is the only holy book."

I was stunned! I'd assumed that Mike was an active follower of Jesus Christ, and that he was about to marry someone who was not a believer. The truth was that Mike and his fiancée were in the same place spiritually. They were both completely adrift. I'm in no place to judge Mike's salvation, but he'd come to the point in his life where there were few if any outward signs of his Christian faith. For me, the realization was deeply disturbing.

At age eighteen, Jenny was a shining star. She had a sterling reputation in her school for being a young woman of character. At our church, she was viewed as a model for younger girls to emulate. She demonstrated a passion for serving others and spent time leading small-group Bible studies. If you had asked me, "Has Jenny been evangelized and discipled?" I would have answered with a resounding, "Yes!" I would have put a check mark next to her name as someone who has clearly and firmly set the course of her life toward following Jesus.

After graduating from high school, Jenny went to a secular college in Washington, DC. When she was a junior in college, she happened to come home on a weekend when I was preaching. That Sunday afternoon, she sent an e-mail to me expressing serious concerns about the content of my sermon. Her fundamental disagreement was that I kept referring to the Bible as "the Word of God." She said that it was offensive to her when I kept using this phrase, as if the Scriptures were the only means of authoritative truth that we had. Again, I was stunned. After further interaction with her, I realized that in three short years she had gone from passionately following Christ to the point where she no longer believed that the Bible was the unique and authoritative Word of God.

Steven was the grandson of career missionaries to Southeast Asia. Not only were his grandparents missionaries, but his great-grandparents, and great-great-grandparents were as well. He had a marvelous and rich spiritual heritage. Steven, however, was not a Christian. He didn't consider himself a religious person at all. When he was growing up, his family never, in fact, went to church. How could this happen? The answer is both simple and tragic.

Steven's mother, the daughter of the third-generation missionaries, rejected her parents' faith. She then raised her children in a nonreligious home. Three generations of men and women had a radical Christian commitment on the mission field, and yet just two short generations later all signs of Christian faith had vanished.

THE CURRENT FAITH-CRISIS

Stories like these are replicating themselves millions of times over in our culture. George Barna's research from 2006 indicates that 80 percent of young adults in their twenties are disconnected from church. Three out of four of these young people *were* connected in church as teenagers but drifted away. Barna surveyed not only church connections for young adults, but also their faith convictions. He set out to discover what percentage of adults in their twenties and thirties expressed a strong commitment to faith in Christ and belief in the Bible. He wanted to determine specifically how many people

Eighty percent of young adults are disconnected from church.

- have made a personal commitment to Jesus Christ;
- view their commitment to Christ as very important in their lives today;
- believe that when they die they will go to heaven because they have confessed their sins and have accepted Jesus Christ as their Savior;
- believe that God wants them to share their faith;
- believe that Satan exists;

- believe that eternal salvation is possible only through grace, not works;
- believe that Jesus Christ lived a sinless life on earth;
- assert that the Bible is accurate in all it teaches;
- describe God as the all-knowing, all-powerful Creator who is actively involved in all things.

Take a moment and reread the list above. Does that list describe you? Barna found these basic benchmarks of biblical Christianity in only 6 percent of young adults in their twenties and thirties.[1]

Researcher Thom Rainer, from Southern Baptist Theological Seminary, affirms this heartbreaking reality. He led a study to determine what percentage of Americans claimed to be Christians based upon having put their faith in Christ. In other words, what percentage of Americans identify themselves as Christians and understand that being a Christian means putting one's faith in Christ alone for salvation? Here's what he found. Among Americans born before 1946, 65 percent identified themselves as Christians and were able to articulate the basics of the gospel. For those born between 1946 and 1964, the number dropped to 35 percent. For those born between 1965 and 1976, it fell to a scant 15 percent. Finally, among Americans born between 1974 and 1994, only 4 percent of the population identified themselves as Christians and had trusted Christ alone for salvation.[2]

Evangelism and discipleship are in dire crisis, and *it is a generational crisis.* We're losing more of our own children to the world than we are winning adult converts to faith in Christ. As a result, the percentage of Bible-believing Christians in the United States is in steady decline. The United States is, in fact, following in the misguided footsteps of Western Europe. The lands that birthed the Reformation are now overwhelmingly secular, with Bible-believing Christians making up just 1 percent of the population in some countries.[3]

How could this have happened? There are many reasons, and we need to understand the past if we hope to lead our children toward a different future. In the remainder of this chapter, we'll explore some of the cataclysmic changes that have rocked Western culture, and how those changes have had an impact on the souls of our sons and daughters.

PHILOSOPHICAL REVOLUTION

The past century has seen a radical and destructive shift in how people think. The shift progressed with each generation, and two key words capture this thought revolution—pluralism and relativism. Pluralism, put simply, is the reality that people have many choices about what they believe. Pluralism has existed since the garden of Eden and is the consequence of living in a world with good and evil. Today, our world is filled with a *plurality* of religions and values from which to choose. Each has its attractions. There are sides. There are differences. But there is truth and there are lies. We're free to choose what we will believe, and God will hold us responsible for those choices.

Today's young people are saturated with pluralism, which has become unfortunately intertwined with relativism. The philosophy of relativism suggests that all statements of fact depend upon one's perspective. In other words, all statements of truth depend upon your point of view, and are relative in comparison to the point of view of others. If we tell someone that we believe Christianity is *true*, we frequently hear the response, "I'm glad that you've found something that works for you. Christianity is true for you, and my beliefs are true for me."

Consider the basic premise of relativism: "All statements of fact are relative." Look carefully at this declaration. There's an immediate problem—if all statements of fact are relative, then no statement of fact is absolutely true. If nothing is absolutely true, then the statement, "All statements of fact are relative," cannot be true either. That statement itself is a pronunciation of fact. Thus, the philosophy of relativism is thoroughly self-defeating. Its basic premise teaches that you cannot accept a basic premise. It is philosophically and logically dead before it even begins, and yet this lie has penetrated the hearts and minds of millions of people around the world.

If you were to dialogue with someone who embraces a relativistic view of the world, it may not be long before he or she brings up the famous parable from India about the blind men and the elephant. Maybe you've heard this one before. A group of three blind men are helping each other feel their way down a path. One of them bumps into an object that is blocking their way. An elephant is standing in middle of the path. The blind men then began to argue with one another about what stands before them. One man has his hand on the side of the elephant and explains that someone built a wall across the path. Another man reaches out and touches the tail. He argues that they're being blocked by a thicket of sticks and branches. The third blind man reaches out and touches the legs. He tries to persuade his friends that they're being blocked by a row of thick trees. Who is correct? This parable is repeated over and over again as an example of how truth depends on our perspective. Each blind man touched a part of the elephant, and from each man's perspective, his report was accurate.

I have yet to fully understand why this parable is used so frequently to defend pluralism and relativism. The moral of this story is not that truth is subjective and depends on each man's perspective. The moral is that each man was objectively wrong. The men were blocked by something in the path. It was not a wall, a thicket, or trees. It was an elephant.

Pluralism and relativism are most deadly when they come together in matters of faith. A few years ago, I met weekly with a group of high school students at a local restaurant. None of them were Christians, and it would be an understatement to say that the group was diverse. All together, they had pierced every pierceable body part, and had every shade of color in their hair. We had a great time every Friday afternoon talking about issues of faith, God, and the Bible. One day I asked them, "Who do you think God is?" A young man with wild hair said, "I think God is kind of like my granddad in Florida. He's there, but I never really see him." Another quickly chimed in, "God is an evil being who's out to punish us and make our lives a living hell."

The third took the opposite tact: "I don't think God exists at all," she said. What would I hear next? "I believe God is everywhere and in everything," said another teen. "He's the rocks. He's the trees. The universe is God. I am God, too." At that point there was an uncomfortable pause. Finally, another student offered his opinion in a thoughtful tone. "You know what? You're all right. You all see God in a way that's true for you, and it works for you."

I expected the other students to either fall out of their seats laughing or find some way to tell this young man that his conclusion was silly. Each student said things that were totally antithetical to one another. One said that God is an evil being who wants to hurt us, another said that there is no God, and still another that *he* is God. But rather than respond with incredulity, everyone around the circle nodded their heads and said, "Yeah. You know what? You're right. We're all right. Each one of us sees the world from our own perspective, and we each have our own truth."

Pluralism offers us every imaginable set of concepts and faith systems. Relativism persuades us that all concepts and systems are equally true and equally valid—all at the same time. This insidious combination has proved to be a devastating philosophical one-two punch in the hearts and minds of our sons and daughters. It's also become a destructive institution in Western culture. The public schools that you likely attended as a child are nothing like the public schools of today. Only a few decades ago, prayer was encouraged in public schools, the Bible could be read comfortably in class, and songs were sung about Jesus the Messiah at the Christmas program. Your children, however, had a dramatically different experience, and you'd likely shudder if you knew what your grandchildren are being exposed to. Today, the curriculum is built upon the principles of pluralism, relativism, atheism, and evolution. Many wonderful Christian teachers and administrators work in our schools today, but it's the curriculum that is shaping the hearts and minds of this generation. Today our curriculum is not neutral toward Christianity—it is diametrically opposed to it.[4]

Science curriculum is built upon the theory of atheistic evolution. To stand up in a public-school science classroom and say, "I believe that God created the world and that human beings are a unique and special creation separate from the animals," is an invitation to ridicule. A second grader in my neighborhood was asked to tell the class who his hero was. He said, "My hero is Jesus." The teacher immediately and sternly announced, "No one is allowed to say that name in this classroom!" The student was both scared and devastated. The teacher, of course, was wrongly applying the laws related to the first amendment of the constitution. Students are allowed to talk freely about their religion in the classroom. It is *teachers* who are restricted from proselytizing. In this case, the parents let the principal know what happened, and the teacher was corrected—but the damage was done.

In the last twenty years, even our youngest students have been pressed upon to reject God's truth and embrace the values of this world. In 1992, Charles Colson called the nation's attention to books that were being given to first graders around the country. *Heather Has Two Mommies* and *Daddy's Roommate* were written to celebrate homosexual relationships and normalize homosexual parenting.[5]

Your children have grown up in a culture steeped in moral pluralism and relativism.

Today, all Americans hear these views espoused from the President of the United States. On September 28, 2009, President Obama gave his Family Day Proclamation, in which he declared, "Whether children are raised by two parents, a single parent, grandparents, a same-sex couple, or a guardian, families encourage us to do our best."[6] When the elected leader of our nation casts aside a fundamental moral principle, we should not be surprised at the chaos that rules our day.

DECAY IN THE CHURCH

Your children, then, have grown up in a culture steeped in moral pluralism and relativism. This philosophical revolution is now wreaking havoc even in our churches. Some Christians are skilled at bashing the secular culture around us, but often turn a blind eye to the destructive forces at work in our churches. Many pockets of the Christian church quietly followed society on a parallel track of decay, and now the seeds that were planted are bearing fruit—the fruit of millions of our children and grand-children far from God.

How has the church been infected by the philosophical revo-lution? We've largely abandoned our belief in the sufficiency of Scripture. The Protestant Reformation was built on the "five solas":

- *Sola fide*—only faith. We are not saved by our good works, but through faith.
- *Sola gratia*—only grace. We do not deserve salvation; it is by the grace of God.
- *Solus Christus*—only Christ. Only through the work of Christ can we be saved.
- *Soli Deo Gloria*—only for the glory of God. The glory of God is the purpose of all things.
- *Sola Scriptura*—only Scripture. The Bible alone is a suf-ficient guide for all matters of faith and practice.

I recently had lunch with Don Cole, who has served as a pas-tor on Moody Radio for many years. I asked him how he would define *sola Scriptura*. He said, "In the Bible we have everything we *need* to know. God has given us everything important, about everything important. In it we find everything that matters, about everything that matters."

Is the Bible a comprehensive guide about science? No. But everything we *need* to know about science is there. God created the universe, for instance. Chance had nothing to do with it. Human beings were created as special and unique, totally dis-tinct from the animals. Everything that matters... about every-thing that matters.

I recently spoke at a Christian high school weekend retreat. They asked me to preach on John 15, the passage where Jesus teaches about the vine and the branches. Jesus' primary call to His disciples in that passage is that they "remain in me." Jesus begins to explain what this means in verse 7 when He says, "If you remain in me and my words remain in you…" Then in verse 10 He makes it plain, "If you obey my commands, you will remain in my love." We spent the weekend talking about the importance of giving our best to obeying God's Word—the Bible.

At the end of the weekend we had a question-and-answer session. A young man asked me a great question: "Can you be a Christian and not go to church? I don't like going to church." A group of students around this young man seemed to share his sentiments. I began my answer this way: "If a person claims to be a follower of Jesus, and is not faithfully involved in the local church, then he or she is a disobedient Christian. I can't comment on anyone's salvation, but in Hebrews 10:25 God says that we should 'not give up meeting together, as some are in the habit of doing.'"

The young man responded, "I get that, but we don't like our church. Here's what we want to do. We're going to meet at our friend's house every Friday night, sing some songs, pray, and talk about Jesus. Our youth pastor told us that church was all about encouraging each other spiritually, so that's what we want to do. What do you think about that?"

I replied, "Wow! I love what you're talking about. You're committing to meet every Friday night with your friends to focus on spiritual growth together? That's terrific. I do have a couple questions for you. First, will there be preaching of the Bible when you meet?"

"No."

"Will you have baptisms?"

"No."

"Will you have communion?"

"No."

"Will you have multiple, biblically qualified elders there?"

"No."

"Again, I don't have anything negative to say about your meeting every week like you described. It sounds wonderful. But... it's not a church. Church is not man's idea. We didn't think it up. Church is God's idea. He's the one who instituted it, and He is the one who gave us, in the Scriptures, the patterns and practices that He wants for it."

"Well, Pastor Rob, where does it say in the Bible that you have to have elders?"

At this point, I confess... I got lucky. I likely wouldn't have known the answer to that question off the top of my head. But God knew that this question would come my way this weekend, and so a few days earlier I "just happened" to be reading in the book of Titus. So I replied, "In Titus 1:5, Paul instructs the church that the first thing they were to do is appoint elders in every town."

At that moment, the young man responded with a question I'll never forget. He said, "How about another one?" In other words, do you have *another* Bible passage that supports what you're saying?

My heart fell inside of me, and I quietly said, "I didn't know I needed more than one." This was a retreat with students who professed faith in Christ. I realized in that moment that this young man and I were not having a disagreement about the nature of church—but rather a disagreement about the nature of the Bible. This young man, like many of his Christian peers, did not view the Bible as a *sufficient* guide for life—in this case, the particular nature and function of the church. He'd asked me a question. I answered his question with a plain Scripture. It wasn't enough to change his mind, nor the minds of many around him. The Bible alone was not enough. Yet, "All Scripture is God-breathed and is useful for teaching, rebuking, correcting and training in righteousness, so that the man of God may be thoroughly equipped for every good work" (2 Tim. 3:16–17).

I frequently ask groups of Christian youth and young adults the following four questions. First, "Do you believe the Bible is God's Word?" All the hands go up. Second, "Do you believe it is completely true?" Again, all the hands show. Now things get dicey. The third question, "Are you willing to submit all your thoughts and opinions on every matter to what it says?" A few hands rise from the crowd. Finally, "Are you willing to do what it says, even if you don't want to?" Again, only a few hands go up. In regard to this last question, I'm not talking about the willful disobedience that we struggle with on a daily basis. On many occasions we know exactly what we're doing, that it's against God's Word, and we choose to do it anyway. Rather, I'm talking about the Christian who says, "I know the Bible says that this isn't right, but I don't think the Bible is completely relevant on this topic."

The twentieth century saw what Francis Schaeffer called a new kind of Christian—a person who claims to be a follower of Jesus Christ, someone who "loves Jesus," but who does not believe the Bible. Millions of young people grew up on an anemic diet of Sunday school Bible stories, and the end result, as they moved into adulthood, was that the Bible remained a nice story with some valuable wisdom. They were neither taught, nor did they embrace the central Christian doctrine of the sufficiency of Scripture for all matters of faith and life. When young people distance their hearts and minds from not only the inerrancy of Scripture but its sufficiency, spiritual deterioration is inevitable.

Pluralism and relativism are no longer found just "out there" in the culture around us; they can frequently be found in the halls and sanctuaries of our churches. But we can easily slip into a mode of blaming the list of outside forces that robbed faith from our children. We bring to mind the non-Christian friends they spent time with, the atheistic professors at college, or the youth pastors that didn't do enough to help. All these influences may be at work, but we must face even deeper issues if we want to embrace the mission of pointing the hearts of our children to Christ.

In this chapter we've considered changes in our culture and in our churches. In the next chapter, we turn our attention to the issues in our own homes.

Questions for Reflection/Discussion

1. What words would you use, positive or negative, to describe your children's generation?
2. Do you believe your children's generation thinks differently than yours? How?
3. In your opinion, what changes have occurred in our public schools from the time you were growing up to today?[7]
4. Can you identify specific issues over which Christians have lost their conviction about the inerrancy and sufficiency of Scripture?

Chapter 2

THE PERFECT STORM

A FEW YEARS AGO a movie was released called *The Perfect Storm*. It told the heroic tale of a ship that encountered a once-in-a-lifetime storm—a perfect storm—that resulted in tragedy. Unbeknownst to the captain of the ship, three separate storms were brewing on the Atlantic, and he was in the wrong place at the wrong time. All three weather systems collided at a single point, creating some of the most violent seas ever recorded.

In the previous chapter we looked at two storms that have been raging in our culture—the philosophy of relativism and the acceptance of pluralism. Within the church, these have contributed to the decline of conviction regarding the sufficiency of Scripture. Now we turn our attention to a third storm that has proven to be the strongest of all—the fragmentation of the family.

THE LOSS OF FAMILY-CENTERED LIFE

During the last one hundred years we've seen a dramatic shift away from an integrated, family-centered style of life to a fragmented, individual-centered lifestyle. This fragmentation now characterizes many neighborhoods, churches, and extended families.

Fragmented Neighborhoods

Many of us grew up in a neighborhood surrounded by people we knew and people who knew us. I knew every one of the twenty families on the street where I was raised. We weren't close friends with all of them, but at age ten I could tell you the name of each family on the block, and I knew them at least well enough to greet them. How many of us live in a neighborhood like that now? Our culture has changed. Many of us barely know the people next door. I'm embarrassed to admit this, but I can stand on my front porch and see houses whose owners I've never even met.

Fragmented Churches

Families have also become fragmented at church. Some churches today are lamenting how the generations in the congregation are segregated from one another into their life-stage ministries. The teens meet with the teens. The senior adults meet with the senior adults. The singles meet with the singles. In some congregations, as soon as a family walks through the front door they scatter to their so-called "age-appropriate" locations. This is neither the biblical nor the historic model for how God's people worship together. Eric Wallace writes,

> The church should be the champion of the family since it is the institution designed by God to nurture and care for families. Despite its many well-intentioned efforts, modern ministry has done very little to help strengthen families. In fact, much ministry has had the opposite effect.... Perhaps we can best measure how the church has failed by looking at the future generation. Are youth today ready to take over leadership in the church tomorrow?[1]

In some cases, church leaders respond to this relational and spiritual fragmentation by initiating multigenerational programming. Church programs are not, however, the root of fragmentation, and therefore they're not the solution. Our local churches merely reflect the generational disconnection of our families. Teens are frequently not close to their own grandparents, so can we expect them to build meaningful relationships with senior adults in their churches? If we want to see multigenerational relationships thrive in the church, we must begin by calling families to live with multigenerational relationships at home.

Fragmented Extended Families

"The stronger the family, the stronger the church; the stronger the church, the more blessed the nation. But have Christian leaders effectively strengthened the vehicle needed to pass along a Christian heritage?"[2]

Research has demonstrated that faith is more likely to thrive in young people when they grow up in the context of integrated family-centered relationships. The most expensive and expansive survey of teenagers and religion was completed in 2005 by Christian Smith. In his book *Soul Searching*, he concludes,

> Those teenagers for whom religious faith and practice are important tend to have religious lives constructed relationally and institutionally to intersect and overlap with other important aspects of their lives. For example, church, family, school, friendships, and volunteer and social activities hang together in an integrated whole.[3]

Families are disconnected from neighbors, fragmented in our churches, and worst of all, separated from one another. Many in your generation grew up with aunts, uncles, and multiple grandparents living nearby. Family gatherings and extended family connections (for better or worse) were seen as a healthy and essential part of family life. Today, family members are often scattered around the country, separated physically, and often emotionally and spiritually as well.

One genealogy Web site, www.ellisisland.org, where you can find the connections to your family history, had twelve billion hits from 2001 to 2008.[4] God built the family to be connected. When it's not, something inside of us longs for it.

When it comes to family fragmentation, older members of the family frequently suffer the most. The message to senior adults in our culture today is, "Your time has passed! It's time for you to move on to a retirement community, and let the next generation take things from here."[5] How far we've fallen from the biblical patriarchal view of family, in which our elders sit in the places of honor and influence. I refuse to believe that it's God's plan for men and women to go through the blessings and trials of life, to learn through painful experiences, to walk with Jesus and know Him in a passionate and personal way, and just when they get to the point of being able to offer some true wisdom and perspectives on life, we tell them their time has passed.

On the other side of the coin, Satan has crafted a second deceptive strategy. He wages his war indirectly, but with firm resolve. He loves for empty-nest parents to believe, "This is my time. I raised my kids. I worked hard. I'm done!" With all due respect to those who have raised their children to adulthood, God's Word calls older

Our responsibilities to lead our families increase—not decrease—when grandchildren come.

men and women to a unique, necessary, and powerful season of ministry and impact. Our responsibilities to lead our families increase—not decrease—when grandchildren come. We may not be changing as many diapers, doing laundry all day, and helping with homework, but if God blesses us with grandchildren, then He has chosen to put more immortal souls under our care and influence—and that is a serious calling from God.

We must all push back against the lie that we no longer have influence in the lives of our children. They may live on the other side of the country and, even worse, their hearts may be very far from us, but the mission of parenting does not end when our kids leave the house. No matter what has happened in our relationships with our sons or daughters, God still has a plan to use us to point their hearts toward Christ.

THE DECLINE OF FAMILY WORSHIP

Did you grow up in a home that practiced family devotions? I v_ asked audiences this question at conferences around the country, and the response is always the same... less than 20 percent of the hands go up. For the current generation of parents in the church, the situation is even worse. Less than one in twenty Christian families have a regular time of worship together at home (Bible reading and prayer together as a family).[6]

If we had asked this question a hundred years ago, we would have found the vast majority of Christian families regularly spent time together reading God's Word, praying with and for one another, and even singing together. For centuries, the Christian church was radically committed to building and nurturing the ultimate discipleship small group—the Christian family. Why was family worship so important and so central to the life of committed believers? Because it was understood that the responsibility for passing the faith to the next generation lay with mom and dad with the help of grandma and grandpa. Believing parents would not have expected the church, a Sunday school teacher, or a youth pastor to be the leader in teaching the Bible to their children. It never crossed their minds that they should try to find a "student small group" or "accountability partner" for their children. They understood, and the church leaders up until that time taught it clearly, that the responsibility for impressing a love for God on the hearts of the next generation rested on the family.

Yet during that era, seeds were planted for what we're reaping today—the modern age of delegation parenting. Our culture has trained my generation that great parents are great at delegating. If I want my kids to learn to play piano, I find a piano teacher. If I want them to learn basketball, I get them a coach. If I want them to learn Jesus, I take them to Sunday school or youth group. My job as the parent is to drive the minivan and make sure that my children are in the best environments to learn all these valuable things. Even church leaders in the last century, rather

parents to lead family worship at home,
...t the most important thing parents could
...n was to have them involved in church pro-
...ou heard this very message from your church
...ur children.

...oviously nothing wrong with piano lessons and
baske... practice. Neither am I putting down children's workers and youth pastors; after all I was a youth pastor for over
a decade and currently oversee all of the children's and youth ministries at our church.[7]

> God created parents to lead, and the church to support, not the other way around.

The point is, the spiritual train-ing of our children and grandchildren is not something that can or should be delegated. God created parents to lead, and the church to support, not the other way around. As I mentioned earlier, however, the decline of family worship is a relatively new development in the Christian community.

Family Worship in History

Up until the late 1800s, family worship was commonly prac-ticed and specifically encouraged by the church. After the Refor-mation, for example, the Presbyterian church in Scotland made family worship a priority. A 1647 Presbyterian document called "The Directory for Family Worship" says,

> The assembly requires and appoints ministers to make diligent search and inquiry, whether there be among them a family or families which neglect the duty of family worship. If such a family is found, the head of the family is to be admonished pri-vately to amend his fault; and in case of his continuing therein, he is to be gravely and sadly reproved by the session; after which reproof, if he is found still to neglect family worship, let him be, for his obstinacy in such an offense, suspended and debarred from the Lord's supper, until he amend.[8]

For these believers, the practice of family worship was so important that it was an issue of church discipline. They understood that if the church was to be serious about making disciples, it had to start with their own children, and that meant parents needed to take the lead at home.

Jonathan Edwards frequently taught on the biblical doctrines of family life. In his 1750 farewell sermon, he wrote,

> We have had great disputes [about] how the church ought to be regulated; and indeed the subject of these disputes was of great importance: but the due regulation of your families is of no less, and, in some respects, of much greater importance. Every Christian family ought to be as it were a little church, consecrated to Christ, and wholly influenced and governed by his rules. And family education and order are some of the chief means of grace. If these fail, all other means are likely to prove ineffectual. If these are duly maintained, all the means of grace will be likely to prosper and be successful.[9]

Charles Spurgeon was writing and preaching in the late 1800s when the steep decline in family worship began. In "The Kind of Revival We Need," he wrote,

> We deeply want a revival of family religion. The Christian family was the bulwark of godliness in the days of the puritans, but in these evil times hundreds of families of so-called Christians have no family worship, no restraint upon growing sons, and no wholesome instruction or discipline. How can we hope to see the kingdom of our Lord advance when His own disciples do not teach His gospel to their own children? Oh, Christian men and women, be thorough in what you do and know and teach! Let your families be trained in the fear of God and be yourselves "holiness unto the Lord"; so shall you stand like a rock amid the surging waves of error and ungodliness which rage around us.[10]

Spurgeon's message is desperately needed today. Godly men and women in growing churches receive the constant call to get involved in ministry. This call is usually a plea for volunteers to help with programs at church. It's a grave mistake, however, to think of ministry as something that we do only outside our homes. My prayer is that God will use your journey through this book to turn your heart toward your most important ministry—doing all in your power to help your children love God with all their hearts!

The Priority of Family Worship at Home

Many Scriptures encourage family worship—the regular gathering of the family for prayer, sharing, and Scripture reading. The primary Scripture is found in Deuteronomy 6, where we find what Jesus in Matthew 22:38 calls, "the first and greatest commandment": "Love the LORD your God with all your heart and with all your soul and with all your strength. These commandments that I give you today are to be upon your hearts" (Deut. 6:5–6).

What would you say if someone asked you, "How are you going to obey the Great Commandment tomorrow?" I know for me there would likely be an awkward pause because this command to love God is a global, all-encompassing, abstract command. Yet in the next few verses God tells us where to start.

Consider verse 7: "Impress them on your children." Here we find the first practical action-point of the Great Commandment. God calls us to do all in our power to impress the hearts of our children with a love for God. You wouldn't be reading this book if that was not the desire of your heart. But how are parents supposed to do this? How can a broken, sinful man like me possibly impress the hearts of my children with a love for God? God tells us where to start as verse 7 continues: "Talk about them when you sit at home and when you walk along the road, when you lie down and when you get up."

So what can parents possibly do to pass faith to our children? Talk! To be more specific, parents are called to talk about the things of God with our children when we sit at home. Consider this section of Scripture as a whole. God begins with the greatest commandment, which is to love Him with all our hearts, and then calls us to a concrete, practical action step—worshipping Him at home with our families.

When God was turning my heart to my family in 2004, I saw this Scripture from Deuteronomy, and I told God in prayer that I didn't have time for family worship because of my busy ministry schedule. Ridiculous, I know! I sensed the conviction of the Holy Spirit, "Rob, the schedule that you have chosen for yourself is causing you to sin by being disobedient to the first thing I have asked you to do as a Christian man—lead Christian worship in your home." It was true.

MY STORY OF REPENTANCE

The summer of 2004 was a dark chapter in my life. My wife, Amy, and I had been blessed with four children. (We now have six.) I'd been serving as a youth minister for over a decade. If you had asked me at that time what my priorities in life were as a Christian man, I would have responded quickly and with conviction, "My first priority in life is my personal relationship with God, followed by my love relationship with my wife. My kids come next, and my fourth priority is my ministry in the church." God, spouse, kids, others. Not only did I preach about this prioritized Christian life, I lived it. If the phone rang and my boss was on the line with a crisis, and at the same time the other phone rang and Amy was on the line with a crisis, where would I go? How would I respond? I would go home. In a crisis, I would not put my work ahead of my wife.

Over the course of that summer, the Holy Spirit began to press me with a difficult question: "What are your priorities if there is no crisis?" During a normal week, where did I give the best of my heart, passion, energy, leadership, and vision? When I considered my life in light of that question, I didn't like what I saw. I preached the Christian life priorities of God, spouse, kids, and others, but in my everyday life, the order was completely backward—others, kids, Amy, God.

It sounds so horrible to say it this way, but my heart was at my job. When I was at work, I was thinking about work. When I was at home, I was thinking about work. My ministry at church was truly my first love.

This was followed by my relationship with my children. I was not an absent father, physically or emotionally. I tried to spend time with them and connect with them personally. But I had no plan whatsoever to pass my faith on to my children. As a youth pastor, I had tremendous strategic plans to pass my faith on to everyone else's children! But with the immortal souls that God had entrusted to my care... I was just showing up. I gave them my spiritual leftovers after I had poured myself out at work.

My next priority was my marriage to Amy. After I gave my best at work and gave the leftovers to the kids, Amy got what few scraps were left. This is not to say that I didn't try to spend time with her and do what I could to help around the house, but my heart was not with her first and foremost. I was seen as a strong spiritual leader at my church while at home I was providing virtually no spiritual encouragement for my wife.

Because my life was totally upside-down and backward, I was also far from God... and I didn't even know it.

It was a dark summer because I had to admit that the life I thought I was living was a mirage. I was not a man who put my ministry to my wife and children first. God brought me to a place of deep brokenness and repentance. I confessed and acknowledged the broken state of my life to God and repented to my wife and children. Then God began to graciously rebuild my family on the firm foundation of His Word and His grand purpose for our lives. I began to lead my family spiritually and began the practice of family worship together at home. It was not too late for me to turn my heart to my family, and it's not too late for you.

NEVER TOO LATE

In the previous two chapters we've looked at some of the changes that have taken place in our culture, churches, and even our families during the last hundred years. As a result, Christian parents of adult children who are struggling with faith are the rule rather than the exception. Millions of other young men and women have taken the same path, or at least ended up in the same place—living a life far from God. But there is good news. God is on His throne! He cares about us, our children, and the generations to come. We are not alone, and it is never too late for God to use us to impress the hearts of our children with a love for Jesus. Our children have one of the greatest blessings in the world—a Christian parent. Our families are not perfect. Our relationships are filled with problems and pain, but we are still family, and God has created the family with transformational power. Consider the words from the nineteenth-century writer Jacob Abbott:

> God has grouped men in families, having laid the foundation of this institution so deep in the very constitution of man that there has been no nation, no age, scarcely even a single savage tribe that has not been drawn to the result which He intended. For thousands of years, this institution has been assailed by every power that could shake it by violence from without, or undermine it by treachery from within. Lust and passion have risen in rebellion against it. Atheism has again and again advanced to the attack, but the Christian family unit stands unmoved. It has been indebted to no human power for its defense. It has needed no defense. The family stands on the firm, sure, and enduring foundation that God has made for it. Wars, famine, pestilence, and revolutions have swept over the face of society carrying confusion, terror, and distress to social structures. Time has undermined and destroyed everything that it could touch, and all human institutions have thus been altered or destroyed in the lapse of ages. But the family lives on; it stands firm and unshaken. It survives every shock, and rises again unharmed after every tempest that blows over the social sky. God created marriage to bless His creatures and to advance His purposes in the

earth, and He has laid its foundations too deep and strong to be removed.[11]

It is now time to turn our attention in the next chapter to the hope we have in Christ, and to the principles in Scripture that can give us encouragement and guidance for the journey ahead.

Questions for Reflection/Discussion

1. In what ways do you see the fragmenting of extended families in our culture today?
2. Do you perceive that your role and influence in your family is growing or decreasing as you age?
3. Did you grow up in a home that practiced family worship? If so, describe the experience. Did you practice family worship when your children lived at home?
4. Why do you think your child is struggling with faith?

Chapter 3

HOPE

CASE STUDY I: DREAMS OF PARENTHOOD

Michael and Jenny fell in love at the tender age of twenty. One of their favorite topics of conversation was the dreams they both shared about children and raising a family. They married a few months after their first date. The day after the wedding, Michael left on a battleship, deployed for service in the war. Two months later, Jenny sent word to her new husband that she was expecting. He was overwhelmed that God had blessed them with a child, but at the same time he was despairing that he wouldn't be home when the baby was born.

Jenny began to develop complications seven months into her pregnancy, and after weeks of bed rest the baby's due date finally came. The delivery went well, but it was soon learned that their precious daughter had a rare genetic condition... one that would take her life after only twenty-four hours. The parents went through their grieving thousands of miles apart.

A year later, Michael was finally able to return home. God again blessed them with a new baby growing inside Jenny. This pregnancy went more smoothly than the first, and there was prayerful anticipation of the blessing to come. This time, they were together in the hospital when the baby came. To their dismay, this child was also ill... and lived only six days.

The shock was overwhelming, and the pain rarely discussed. After some months went by, they felt the Lord leading them to build a family through adoption. God provided them with the opportunity to raise both a daughter and a son—Julie and Jeff. The dream of parenthood had become reality. But as Jeff entered high school, their dream family began to fall apart at the seams. The rift began with Jeff's little lies about where he was going, then some money came up missing from Dad's bedroom drawer. The situation escalated into their son using drugs and, at times, staying away from home for days at a time. Today, their son is in his thirties and is in federal prison, having been convicted of sex crimes against a child.

Julie lives one state away and has children of her own. She and her parents have a pleasant relationship... unless Michael or Jenny try to talk about their faith in Christ. Julie has strongly proclaimed herself to be agnostic, and has made it clear that she is not comfortable talking with her parents about all that "religious stuff."

As I listened to this couple tell me their story, I fully expected it to come to an awkward and hopeless ending. But by God's grace, Michael and Jenny have continued to pursue the hearts and souls of their children. They faithfully write to their son in prison, and he now writes back. In almost every letter they receive from him, he writes things like, "I love you." "I'm sorry for the choices I made." "Thanks for loving me." He is now attending Bible studies and is on his own journey toward Christ.

While their daughter expresses no interest in faith conversations, they continue to pursue a relationship with her, and especially with her three children. When their grandchildren are with them, they talk openly about their faith, about the Bible, and the goodness of God.

God is on the move in this precious family. Despite a difficult past, it was not too late for God to use Michael and Jenny to encourage faith in their grown children, and now in their grandchildren.

CASE STUDY 2: THE PREACHER'S KID

When I was nineteen, I decided I'd be honest and stop saying I was a Christian. At first I pretended that my reasoning was high-minded and philosophical. But really I just wanted to drink gallons of cheap sangria and sleep around. Four years of this, and I was strung out, stupefied, and generally pretty low. Especially when I was sober or alone.

My parents—strong believers who raised their kids as well as any parents I've ever seen—were brokenhearted and baffled. I'm sure they wondered why the child they tried to raise right was such a ridiculous screw-up now. But God was in control.

One morning, before eight o'clock, I went to the library to check my e-mail. I had a message from a girl I'd met a few weeks before. Her e-mail mentioned a verse in Romans. I went down to the Circle K and bought a forty-ounce can of Miller High Life. Then I went back to where I was staying, rolled a few cigarettes, cracked open my drink and started reading Romans. I wanted to read the verse from the e-mail, but I couldn't remember what it was, so I started at the beginning of the book. By the time I got to chapter 10, the beer was gone, the ashtray needed emptying and I was a Christian.

The best way I know to describe what happened to me that morning is that God made it possible for me to love Jesus. When He makes this possible and at the same time gives you a glimpse of the true wonder of Jesus, it's impossible to resist his call.[1]

This is the story of Abraham Piper, son of Pastor John Piper. He was the prodigal son, now safely home.

OUR JOURNEY AHEAD

Three messages will be repeated throughout this book. Each of them is vital for the calling that God has given to us, which is to do all in our power to encourage faith in our children.

First, if your child is among those who are wayward, you are not alone. Millions of your brothers and sisters in Christ know the same pain, despair, and fear that you have experienced. You know the discouragement, guilt, and sleepless nights that come when one of your own children or grandchildren is far from God. If the statistics are accurate, the majority of empty-nest Christian parents have at least one child who is not a believer, or who is not walking with the Lord. Through the surveys I've conducted at Wheaton Bible Church and at our Never Too Late conferences, we've discovered that two out of every three of our empty-nest parents are in this situation.

No matter what has happened in our relationships with our sons or daughters, how we were raised, or the choices we made as parents—it's never too late for God to use us to point our children to Christ.

Therefore, many others in your church likely share the same pain, confusion, anger, and helplessness. Most parents, though, suffer in silence. For some, the pain is too great to share. Some feel ashamed to admit that they have a wayward child. For others, it's just easier to live their lives as best they can, trying not to think about the eternal consequences for their children. They "don't go there." I pray that you'll share the journey of this book with your friends. You're going to need a lot of prayer and support, and I'm confident that you have friends who are in the same situation. You need each other.

The second message is, it's never too late. As long as you and your son or daughter still has breath, God can use your relationship with your child to point him or her toward a saving faith and life-transforming relationship with Christ. No matter what has happened in our relationships with our sons or daughters, how we were raised, or the choices we made as parents—it's never too late for God to use us to point our children to Christ. God loves our families, and He loves our children. May His truth inspire our hearts, fill us with hope, give us courage, and prepare us for action.

Third, hold fast to the goal. One of the enemy's primary objectives in the lives of Christians is to distract us from the things that matter most. He always seeks to pull our hearts away from the Lord, and away from approaching our lives with an eternal perspective. It's essential for us to be clear about what we want, or better yet what God wants. Here's my best expression of the goal that we need to keep before us:

> Our children loving God with all of their hearts, putting their full faith and trust in Jesus for their present and their future, and arriving safely home together with us in heaven.

Take a moment right now and write the name of your child on the line below. After you do that, read this short prayer to the Lord:

> Lord, it is my dream and prayer that _____ would love you wholeheartedly, trust Jesus for his/her present and future, and that we would arrive together, safely home in heaven.

THE SHORTEST DISTANCE

How could this dream ever become reality? For many of you, even putting these words together in the form of a prayer may seem impossible. And, indeed, this dream would be impossible if we sought to accomplish it in our own strength. This dream can only come to pass if God's grace and power work in our hearts, and in the hearts of our children. That is exactly what we're going to ask Him, in faith, to do. Prayer plays a central role in encouraging faith in our children.

God's Word calls us to more, however, than prayer. That sounds very unspiritual, I know. In no way do I want to minimize the importance or power of prayer, but the Scriptures give us not only a *prayer* plan, but an *action* plan to reach the hearts of our children. Praying for them without actively and personally seeking to point their hearts to Christ is like praying for God to give us the money to pay the bills, without our ever going out to look for work. Only God's grace and power can bring a child to salvation, and for that purpose God has ordained mothers and fathers as His primary instruments.

I'm convinced that the shortest distance between the heart of your child and faith in Christ is you. Is it possible that God will lead your child to a vibrant faith in Christ apart from you? Yes. Could it be that the Lord has a plan to bring someone else into your child's life who will encourage him or her to trust Christ? Certainly. Should we be praying for the Lord to use anyone and everyone to help our children follow God? Absolutely. But the way that God designed for children to come to Him is through their relationships with their parents. It's the easiest and shortest route. No matter how strained, broken, or distant our relationships with our children, God has the power to use us and our unique roles as mothers or fathers to help them arrive safely home.

FOUR BIBLICAL PRINCIPLES

In the previous chapter, we saw how confidence and belief in the Bible has eroded and how that erosion has had a tragic effect on younger generations. We don't want to make the mistake, then, of neglecting Scripture when trying to reach our wayward children. In the coming chapters, you won't find the latest tips, tricks, and research on effective strategies for parenting an adult child. If the Bible gives us everything important about everything important, then we want to go to the pages of Scripture with this pressing question: How can we as parents encourage faith in our children? We can give thanks that God gives us clear and compelling answers to this question. We're not left on our own to figure it out. I believe that we can summarize God's call to parents with four principles:

- *Offer your heart to the Lord.* God leads us to begin this journey in our own hearts and in our personal relationships with Him. We'll talk about our struggle with guilt, the power of prayer, and our need for repentance.

- *Turn your heart to your child.* When we draw near to the Lord, He increasingly turns our hearts to our children. He awakens in us an overwhelming sense of mission and calling to encourage faith in them. We'll talk about our need to pray for a spirit of compassion for our children, and how we may need to forgive our children for ways they've hurt us.

- *Draw your child's heart to yours.* If the shortest distance between your child's heart and Christ is your relationship with your son or daughter, then you want to rebuild and restore your "heart-connection" with your child. We'll explore how to restore honesty, openness, and trust with our sons and daughters.

- *Point your child's heart to Christ.* As God restores and rebuilds our relationships, we increasingly have opportunities to have spiritual conversations and interactions. We'll address specific ways to approach talking about faith in ways that invite engagement, rather than cause division.

These biblical principles pave our path ahead. We'll look to the Scriptures to understand God's direction, and then talk about how to apply it in our own relationships with Him and with our children. Is this a magic formula? Not at all. I wish there was one. There are no guarantees. Our children are on spiritual journeys, and the last miles have not yet been travelled.

What we can say for sure is that our calling and mission is not to sit idly by and wait to see what happens. God calls us to personally engage and to do all in our power to help our children know God, love Him, and arrive safely home. This is our most important mission in this life. We can be thankful that we don't need to come up with a creative strategy. God has already gone before us and given us clear principles in Scripture. So let's trust Him and start with the directions He has given us.

Questions for Reflection/Discussion

1. If so many empty-nest parents in the church today have adult children who are far from God, why are so few people talking about it?

2. When did you first see indications that your son or daughter was struggling with faith?

3. Is it hard for you to believe that the shortest distance between your child's heart and Christ is you? Why or why not?

Chapter 4

OFFER YOUR HEART TO THE LORD

You're reading this book because you're concerned about the soul of your son or daughter. But before we can have an impact on our children, we must first look at our own hearts. God has a lot to say about parenting in the Scriptures, and He tells us first to offer our own hearts to Him.

In a previous chapter we looked at the Great Commandment found in Deuteronomy: "Love the LORD your God with all your heart and with all your soul and with all your strength. These commandments that I give you today are to be upon your hearts. Impress them on your children" (6:5–7).

So the first mission God gives to His people is to impress the hearts of their children with a love for God. But look at what comes first. "Love the LORD *your* God with all *your* heart and with all *your* soul and with all *your* strength. These commandments that I give you today are to be upon *your* hearts." Only after God's call for us to offer our hearts to Him does He then call us to impress the hearts of our children with this same love for God. We cannot lead our children in a direction we are not ourselves going. Consider some of the final words of Moses that he spoke to the people of Israel: "Take to heart all the words I have solemnly declared to you this day, so that you may command your children to obey carefully all the words of this law" (Deut. 32:46).

Once again, God calls us to look at our own hearts, and then the hearts of our children. As parents, the first and most important thing we must do is *take to heart all the words* that God has spoken to us in Scripture. Why is this so vital? Why does it matter where our hearts and minds are when it comes to God and His word? According to this text, we take to heart all the words of the Lord so that we may lead our children to love and obey God. This doesn't mean that parents must become perfect people before we can have a spiritual impact on our children. Rather, we must be able to come to our children with an authentic heart and say to them, "It's the desire of my heart to love God and follow Him all the days of my life. By God's grace, this is the journey that I'm on. _____, I want to invite you to join me in this journey."

TWO EXTREMES

In my conversations with empty-nest parents around the country, I've frequently found two extreme perspectives on the role and responsibility that these parents have in their children's spiritual waywardness. On one end of the spectrum are those parents who feel completely responsible and 100 percent to blame for their grown children who are not walking with the Lord. For these parents, it's all their fault. They replay their parenting mistakes over and over in their minds. If only they had chosen a Christian school. If only they had spent more time with their children. If only they had seen the warning signs. If only... if only. This is the "total responsibility" extreme.

On the other end of the spectrum are those parents who have told me, "We did the best job we could as parents. We weren't perfect, but we did a good job. Kids are going to make their own decisions. I can't take any responsibility for the choices my children have made. They've taken their own paths." This is the "no responsibility" extreme.

Total
Responsibility   ←—|—|—|—|—|—|—|—|—→   No
Responsibility

I imagine you have friends who are in the same situation you are. At which end of this spectrum do you think most parents fall? Do your peers tend to take total responsibility or no responsibility for how their adult children have turned out? What about you? Perhaps you wouldn't be completely on one side or the other, but which way would you tend to lean?

Total Responsibility

The truth is not found at either end of the spectrum. For those who tend to be on the left side—taking total responsibility for their adult children's lack of faith—the Scriptures are clear that every child is an independent person. A child is a free moral agent, and when it comes to salvation and a relationship with God, the decision in response to the grace of God rests with the child.

God's Word speaks plainly to this issue in Ezekiel 18:20, where we read, "The soul who sins is the one who will die. The son will not share the guilt of the father, nor will the father share the guilt of the son. The righteousness of the righteous man will be credited to him, and the wickedness of the wicked will be charged against him."

We're all born into families, but each person stands alone before God.

In other words, if a father is a righteous man who believes in God, his faith and salvation do not automatically transfer to his child. In the same way, if a father is a wicked man who rejects God, his lack of faith and resulting damnation do not automatically transfer to his child. We're all born into families, but each person stands alone before God.

We must guard our hearts against taking total responsibility for the spiritual lives of our children. The enemy will likely tempt you to believe this lie. He may bombard you with negative thoughts:

- My children are much worse than my friends' children.
- My children hate me and will never want anything to do with me.

- My children will never to listen to anything I have to say.
- I have lost my chance to make an impact.

When these and other thoughts invade our minds, we must fight back in prayer. When these discouraging attacks come, you can pray, "God, I reject this lie. I reject this temptation in the name of Jesus. Your Word tells me that I am not totally responsible for the choices my children have made, and it's never too late for You to use me to make a difference in their lives."

No Responsibility

In the same way that the Scriptures prevent us from taking total responsibility for the spiritual lives of our children, we're warned away from the other extreme as well. Can we really say that we had nothing to do with how our children have turned out? Some on this end of the spectrum seem to believe that faithfulness in parenting, or the lack thereof, is irrelevant to who their children grew up to be. God's Word, though, prevents us from shirking all responsibility for the spiritual choices our children make. Consider the second of the Ten Commandments: "You shall not make for yourself an idol in the form of anything in heaven above or on the earth beneath or in the waters below. You shall not bow down to them or worship them; for I, the LORD your God, am a jealous God, punishing the children for the sin of the fathers to the third and fourth generation of those who hate me, but showing love to a thousand [generations][1] of those who love me and keep my commandments" (Exod. 20:4–6).

Two extraordinary spiritual principles are at work here. The first one is mentioned at the end of verse 5: "I, the LORD your God, am a jealous God [which means I want you all for myself, because that is what you were created for], punishing the children for the sin of the fathers to the third and fourth generation of those who hate me."

Perhaps the best way to understand this passage is to talk about generational patterns. Generational patterns are behaviors and character traits that run in family trees. Divorce runs in family trees—it spreads and multiplies. Why? Because parents pass a spiritual legacy to their children and their grandchildren, and that legacy influences them. Abuse runs in family trees. Psychology will never adequately explain why someone who was abused as a child is likely to become an abuser himself. Psychology does play a part, but a family's spiritual legacy draws a picture of how particular sins infect family trees. Destructive legacies and influences like alcoholism, favoritism, and laziness are frequently passed from one generation to another.

Parents pass a spiritual legacy to their children and their grandchildren.

We see destructive family patterns at work through the earliest families in the Bible. In the book of Genesis we find deceit, favoritism, greed, lust—and more—replicating themselves from parent to child to grandchild. Take a moment and think about what unhealthy patterns can be found in your family tree.[2]

God has set a law in place that "a man reaps what he sows" (Gal. 6:7). If you plant a seed, you do not harvest the fruit the next day. There's always a delay between sowing the seed and reaping the fruit. We don't like to think about it, but there are times when we sow sinful choices into our lives and the results appear a generation later. Our children and grandchildren are the ones who may eat the fruit. In Exodus 20:4–6, God says that even grandchildren and great-grandchildren (third and fourth generation) can reap what *we* sow. We must reject the lie that our lives don't affect the lives of the generations that come after us.

Before we get too discouraged, go back with me to Exodus 20. After God tells us about destructive generational patterns, He gives us an amazing promise: But I show "love to a thousand [generations] of those who love me and keep my commandments" (Exod. 20:5–6).

A thousand generations! This is a promise right in the middle of the Ten Commandments from God to you. The choices that we make every day affect our children—no matter how old they are—our grandchildren, our great-grandchildren, and beyond. The power of sin spreads a few generations, but the power of righteousness knows no bounds. When we begin to understand that our lives have a ripple effect through the generations to come, we can increasingly live with a multigenerational mission and vision.

TWO EXTREMES—SAME RESULT

Parents who are on opposite ends of the responsibility spectrum often end up in the same place. Parents on the end of total responsibility find themselves paralyzed with guilt. They're so burdened by the weight of their regret that it paralyzes them, and as a result they are doing little or nothing *now* to reach out and encourage faith in their adult children. Parents on the other end, the extreme of no responsibility, are often passive. They don't see that they had a significant role in shaping their children's faith, so why should they bother exerting effort now?

Total Responsibility	No Responsibility
Filled with Guilt	Passive
No Action *Now*	No Action *Now*

Both groups thus end up making little effort *here and now* to point the hearts of their children toward Christ. As we've seen, though, God's Word calls us away from those extremes, and He has given us direction that pulls us toward the center—our center in Him.

COUNTERACT FEELINGS OF TOTAL RESPONSIBILITY WITH PRAYER

Let's push back first on the unbiblical extreme of taking total responsibility for the choices our children have made. Many of our children's choices have nothing to do with us. Many times we pleaded with them not to take a certain path, and they took it anyway. We don't control our children, nor can we systematically manufacture faith in their hearts. Yet we desire to see them turn from the path they're on and follow Jesus. What do Christians do when we desperately want to change something that we have no control over? We pray! We pray with desperation, and we ask others to pray. We humbly come before the God of the universe and present our requests to Him. We ask Him to do what only He can do—turn the hearts of our children toward Himself. We reject the extreme of total responsibility and respond by asking God to do what we cannot.

Total Responsibility
↓
Filled with Guilt
↓
~~No Action~~ ~~Now~~ PRAYER

I frequently hear empty-nest parents share prayer requests about their wayward children. "Please pray for my son; he's looking for a new job." "Would you pray for my daughter? She's having a hard time in her marriage." "If you think of it, can you say a prayer for our kids? They're having financial problems." These prayers are all well and good. As parents, we care about our children's jobs, marriages, and finances. I think we share prayer requests like these because our hearts are with our children and we want the best for them... but requesting prayer for what we *really* want hurts too much.

If your son or daughter is far from God, make that the focus of your prayers.

Many of you have children who have not put their faith and trust in Christ for the forgiveness of their sins. How often do you ask your friends to pray for your children to repent, believe in Jesus, and be saved? It's rare to have a parent come up to me and say, "Rob, would you please pray for the salvation of my son?" I want to challenge you to pray for what you *really* want. If your son or daughter is far from God, make that the focus of your prayers. Do you remember the goal we talked about earlier?

> Our children loving God with all of their hearts, putting their full faith and trust in Jesus for their present and their future, and arriving safely home together with us in heaven.

If this is your heart's desire, then ask God to accomplish it. Ask others to pray for it as well. Keep praying for the job, the marriage, and the finances—but keep your prayers focused on the goal.

I encourage you to begin the practice of a daily prayer along these lines. Write out this prayer in your own words and put it in a place where you'll see it every day.

> Dear Lord, I lift up the soul of _____ to you. I pray, in the name of Jesus, that _____ would repent and trust fully in Jesus Christ for forgiveness. I pray that _____ will love you wholeheartedly and will live in such a way as to advance your Kingdom on this earth. Most of all, I pray that by your grace, we would all arrive safely home in heaven together.

COUNTERACT FEELINGS OF NO RESPONSIBILITY WITH REPENTANCE

Prayer is the antidote to the deceptive extreme of taking total responsibility for the paths our children have taken. Repentance is the antidote to the other extreme of taking no responsibility. Are we totally responsible for the spiritual state of our children? No. Are we partially responsible? Yes. What do we do when we look back and wish we'd done some things differently? We repent. Repenting is not about wallowing in the past. Rather, we admit and acknowledge the wrong things we have done, and seek forgiveness for them.

When I share the message of this book at conferences, I ask the audience a series of three questions:

- How many of you were perfect parents? (No hands go up.)
- How many of you did some things wrong as a parent? (If you didn't raise your hand for the first question, then you have to raise your hand for this one!)
- Can you name the things you did wrong?

The first question is easy. Am I a perfect parent? Of course not! No one is perfect. We all make mistakes. The second question is a bit more unsettling. Did I do some things wrong as a parent? It sounds harsh to use the word *wrong*. *Mistakes* comes across better, doesn't it? I'm amazed at how few Christian adults are able to utter the words, "I was wrong." We say things like, "I'm sorry for our miscommunication," or, "I'm sorry your feelings were hurt." We all sin, we all do things wrong, but it's a rare confession indeed that includes the heartfelt words, "I was wrong."

The final question is invasive. I don't ask people to answer that one publicly, but to consider the question privately in their hearts. Admitting that we are not perfect... we can handle that one. Admitting that we did things that were wrong... a little harder to swallow, but we can do it. But can we name those things? In the quietness of our hearts, can we look back at some of the decisions that we made as parents and say, "I was wrong," or, "I did the wrong thing."

Repenting of the past does not mean wallowing in it. Repenting does not mean beating ourselves up until we've paid our dues. But as we move forward in our journey together through this book, God's Word is going to challenge us to move forward in encouraging faith in our adult children. Sometimes in order to move forward, we need to deal with our past. If we're dragging a ball and chain behind us, it's hard to run ahead. We must reject the extreme of no responsibility, while we accept partial responsibility and repent of the things that we did wrong as a parent.

No Responsibility

↓

Passive

↓

~~No Action Now~~ REPENTANCE

Representative Repentance

My prayer is that this book will motivate action. If you don't take the biblical principles of parenting and turn them into action, then you're wasting your time. This may mean that you'll need to take a break from reading in order to spend time in prayer, write a letter to your child, or dig deeper into the Bible. I pray, too, that as we explore this first action step of repentance, you'll act on it.

We're going to examine two types of repentance in the Scriptures: representative repentance and individual repentance. Representative repentance is a largely forgotten concept in the church today. Earlier, we talked about the problem of generational sins in family trees. We may not have committed the particular sin that runs in our family tree, yet we can come to God as a representative of our family and, on behalf of the family, confess the sin to God and seek His healing.

We find examples of representative repentance numerous times in the Bible. In Isaiah 6, the prophet Isaiah comes before the Lord and is undone by His holiness. He cries out, "Woe to me… I am ruined! For I am a man of unclean lips, and I live among a people of unclean lips, and my eyes have seen the King, the LORD Almighty" (v. 5). Isaiah confesses not only his own sin, but repents of the sins of the people of Israel.

The prophet Jeremiah also repents to God as a representative of the people of Israel: "Although our sins testify against us, O LORD, do something for the sake of your name. For our backsliding is great; we have sinned against you" (Jer. 14:7). He confesses and seeks forgiveness, not just for himself, but for his brothers and sisters.

Daniel exemplifies this spiritual practice as well. He believed that God would restore the people of Israel to the Promised

Land, and so he sought God in prayer. Daniel prayed and confessed, "O Lord, the great and awesome God, who keeps his
covenant of love with all who love him and obey his commands,
we have sinned and done wrong. We have been wicked and have
rebelled; we have turned away from your commands and laws"
(Dan. 9:4–5).

These men came before God in prayer and confessed the
sins of their people. They came as representatives of a larger
group, confessing the sins of the entire group to the Lord. In
many of these cases, the individual praying was not guilty of the
sin being confessed. Did Daniel turn away from God and reject
the Scriptures? Absolutely not! Yet Daniel, as a representative
of the people of Israel, humbled himself and confessed, seeking
the mercy of God.

I've had to practice representative repentance in my family in regard to our generational pattern of unbiblical divorce.
Between my biological parents and my four siblings, there are
twelve marriages and eight divorces. Many years ago my brother
and I prayed together, "Lord, we come to you as representatives of our family. We are here to confess to you the pattern of
unbiblical divorce in our family tree. We repent of this. We ask
that you would apply the cross of Christ to the generations of
our family and set us free from this sinful pattern. Please end
this pattern in our generation, and in the generations to come."
God has answered that prayer.

My mother also put this principle into practice. She told me
the story of how when my brother and I were boys, she came into
our rooms one night when we were sleeping to pray for us. She
prayed that God would break any pattern of adultery, divorce,
and alcoholism in our lives, and that God would bless each of us
with a future wife who was free from these things as well. The
Lord graciously answered her prayer.

Take a moment now and consider the unhealthy patterns
in your family tree. You may want to take some time with a
family member or a Christian friend and talk about this issue
with that person. When we look at the families in the Bible,

we find all kinds of generational patterns including favoritism, laziness, arrogance, greed, anger, and involvement with false religions. What patterns do you see in your family? Can you name them? You may want to write down your thoughts in a journal and, after identifying some of these generational patterns, do spiritual battle against them by practicing representative repentance.

The Power of a Praying Parent by Stormie Omartian is an excellent resource for parents who want to engage in the spiritual battle for the souls of their children. She encourages parents to actively pray against generational patterns this way:

> Lord, You have said in Your Word that a good man leaves an inheritance to his children's children (Prov. 13:22). I pray that the inheritance I leave to my children will be the rewards of a godly life and a clean heart before You. I ask that wherever there is a sinful trait in me that I have acquired from my family, deliver me from it now in the name of Jesus. I confess my sins to You and I ask for forgiveness and restoration, knowing Your Word says, "If we confess our sins, He is faithful and just to forgive us our sins and to cleanse us from all unrighteousness" [1 John 1:9 NKJV]. I know that cleansing from sin through confession lessens the possibility of passing the habit of sin on to my child. If there is any work of the enemy in my past that seeks to encroach upon the life of my child, I pray against it now by the power and authority given me in Jesus Christ. I pray that my child will not inherit any sin trait from our earthly family. Thank You, Jesus, that in You the old has passed away and all things are new.[3]

Individual Repentance

Identifying generational patterns in our family trees is important, but we must also take the path of personal repentance. This is not about beating ourselves up. It's about offering our hearts to the Lord. In an earlier chapter I shared about the deep repenting I had to do as a father in the summer of 2004. For so many years my heart was with my work more than with my wife and children. I gave my best to helping people grow spiritually at church while I gave my scraps to nurturing faith in the souls of my family. I was leading the men's ministry at our church at the time, and during numerous situations I'd strike up a conversation with a man and soon discover that he was facing a significant challenge in his life. Perhaps he'd lost his job. I'd invite him out to coffee that week, and we'd open God's Word together and pray for each other. I'd often meet multiple times with someone to walk through the valley with him. My calendar was filled with time that I had set aside to meet with people to do all I could to encourage faith in them.

One day that summer, the Lord pressed my heart with the question, "Rob, when was the last time you spent an hour with your own son? When was the last time you read the Bible with him, took time to pray with him, and encouraged his faith?" Can you see what I was doing? I was investing in everyone... except the souls that God had entrusted into my care at home. I was giving my heart and soul to my spiritual opportunities, while I was neglecting my spiritual responsibilities. I had to face this reality in my life and repent. Individual repentance is never fun, but God has innumerable blessings waiting for us on the other side.

I wish I could say that after my summer of repentance I was able to put all this repentance stuff behind me. As a human, though, I have the unfortunate habit of sinning! I keep doing things wrong as a husband and father. Repentance is a constant and needed companion on my journey. I wish this was not the case, but I don't think a week goes by that I don't lose my cool. I raise my voice with my kids, and sometimes speak harshly to them. What do I do after sinning in this way? I repent—first to God and then to my children. It's an advantage in this particular area to have small children. When I raise my voice or speak harshly to my seven-year-old son, JD, he runs into his room and curls up on his bed. I get instant feedback that I hurt my son. I'm able to go to him and say, "JD, I yelled at you. That was wrong of Daddy. I'm so sorry.

Will you please forgive me?" I pray that my family will become experts at asking for, and granting, forgiveness.

Remember the three questions earlier in the chapter? (1) Were you a perfect parent? (2) Did you do things wrong as a parent? (3) Can you name those things? However you answer the third question, those are the things to take to God in humble repentance.

Perhaps you fathers were not obedient to Ephesians 6:4, where God says, "Fathers, do not exasperate your children; instead, bring them up in the training and instruction of the Lord." It may be that you never had family worship in your home, and that you didn't take the lead in teaching the Bible to your children. So what can you do about that now? Your children are grown and gone. You can't turn back the clock and try again. But you can repent.

You can't turn back the clock and try again. But you can repent.

Perhaps others of you reading this book didn't love your spouse the way a Christian man or woman should. As a wife, perhaps your heart was with your friends, the children, or your ministry at church rather than with your husband. Perhaps you didn't show him proper respect. As a husband, perhaps you felt it was your job just to bring home the money, and you abdicated to your wife the responsibility of spiritual leadership of the children. Perhaps you didn't love your wife above all others. Perhaps you gave your children an angry home, anger that flowed out of a hurting marriage.

Some of you may look back and realize that you raised Pharisees. You were obsessed with your children's performances, grades, punctuality, manners, and athletics... but you never paid attention to the matters of the heart. As a result, you have high-performing adult children. Your children may have graduated near the top of their classes. They're making their mark in the world... but their hearts are far from you and far from God.

Perhaps you didn't honor your own parents. Maybe your children saw this as they were growing up. When we sow the seeds of dishonor with our parents, we often reap dishonor from our children. Maybe you were so afraid of your kids' not liking you that you overindulged them. You gave them everything and anything, and as a result they have an attitude of entitlement.

My point is not to accuse you or rub your nose in the past. We all have problems facing our sins. The last thing in the world Satan wants parents to do is be honest with themselves about the things they've done wrong, because when we repent, God sets us free!

For some people, repentance is fine, as long as they don't have to get specific. I recently preached a sermon from the book of Colossians where God says, "See to it that no one takes you captive through hollow and deceptive philosophy, which depends on human tradition and the basic principles of this world rather than on Christ" (Col. 2:8).

I explained this text and then offered some specific examples about how Christians today are being taken captive by worldly philosophies. I suggested that the hollow philosophy of tolerance has invaded many churches, with the end result being Christians who no longer proclaim the gospel and grace of God to a dying world. I shared my concern that many of my Christian peers were, on one hand, saying that they believed life began at the moment of conception, but when it came to voting, they felt that abortion should not be a focal issue. If a candidate espoused the position that a mother had the right to kill her five-year-old child, would you be able to overlook such a position even if you agreed with the candidate on every other issue? Of course not. It would be a clear moral litmus test. Yet, because worldly ways of thinking have indeed invaded the church, there are many Christians who are privately pro-life yet vote pro-abortion. After the message, a well-meaning congregation member said to me, "Rob, your sermon was fantastic! I was tracking with you the whole way... until you started giving examples of hollow and deceptive philosophies. That part made me mad." As long as I was talking in vague generalities, everything was fine. As long as I kept God's Word back in its context two thousand years ago, that was fine. It was a little too invasive to apply God's Word to the here and now.

General repentance accomplishes nothing. We experience the transformational freedom of God when we confess our specific sins to Him. I encourage you to take a break from your reading at this point. Get out a sheet of paper or open your journal. Ask God to reveal to you anything in your past that you need to confess before Him.

As we move ahead in our journey, the Lord will be calling us to run after the souls of our sons or daughters. In order to respond to His call, we need God to set us free from the past. Take some time now for the practice of individual repentance. If you have trusted Christ as your Savior, the grace of God awaits. He is eager to set you free, so that you can reach out to your children with more love and truth than ever before.

Questions for Reflection/Discussion

1. What concept in this chapter made the greatest impact on you?
2. Toward which extreme—taking total responsibility or taking no responsibility—do you lean?
3. What are some practical ways you can begin praying more for your adult child's spiritual life?
4. Have you ever considered practicing representative repentance for the unhealthy patterns in your family tree? How might you put this principle into action during the coming week?

Chapter 5

TURN YOUR HEART TO YOUR CHILD

JOHN WAS ADOPTED INTO a loving Christian family. His father was an elder in their strong, traditional, Bible-teaching church. It was expected that John would simply follow in the footsteps of his parents. Week after week, John attended church and rubbed shoulders with godly people, but he became increasingly disinterested in spiritual things. As a teenager, John claimed to believe in Jesus, and that He died for his sins, but he had no personal relationship with Christ, and his choices were not driven by God's Word.

From time to time, John's parents asked him how things were going in his walk with God. Sometimes he'd give vague but positive answers to pacify them, and other times express irritation at their invasive questioning. He played the part of the Christian teen... until he could make his escape.

In his early twenties, he had his chance. He was now a young adult, and his parents no longer required him to go to church, so he stopped. His parents became increasingly concerned about what he was doing, who he was with, and where he was heading. John's mom and dad felt more pain and fear for him than they showed. They continued to invite him to church with them, but weren't pushy about it.

John drifted away from faith and family, and soon found himself driven by the desires of the moment. He became increasingly entangled in drugs and promiscuity. If he wanted it, he went searching for it. The more he allowed his passions to rule him, the more he withdrew from his relationship with his parents. Their lifestyle, values, and perspectives were totally opposite his and his friends'.

Despite John's headlong pursuit of sin, his parents always had their hearts turned toward him. They continued to call him and sought to include him in family activities. They didn't directly confront him about his lifestyle, even though John secretly wished that they would. Underneath his fast-lane life, you see, John was struggling with guilt and shame, so he avoided anyone who would judge him or call his behavior into question.

Yet his parents kept expressing their warmth and love for him, and when he made good decisions, they went out of their way to praise and encourage him. So even though John knew that his parents didn't approve of his choices, he also knew they loved him. John remembers his parents telling him over and over again, "We're praying for you." As the pain and emptiness of John's life increased, his heart began to soften, and he began to accept more invitations to spend time with his parents.

A few years later, John reconnected with a young woman that he used to see at parties. She wasted no time in telling him that she was now a Christian and invited him to attend church with her. It was somewhat of a surprise to both of them when he accepted. The church service was honest, basic, and Bible-driven—and the Holy Spirit began to lead John's heart back to Jesus. He quickly told his parents that he'd been to church, that it had a big impact on him, and that he'd be going back next week. His parents were cautiously excited. After years of seeing their son descend into the chaos of drug abuse, they didn't want to foolishly look at this one church attendance through rose-colored glasses.

In the coming weeks, John's parents continued to reach out to him. They said things like, "Whenever you're ready to talk, we're here." They also started sharing with John about the things that God was teaching them... both their struggles and their joys. The more they shared their hearts and struggles with John, the more freedom he felt to open up his heart in return. His deepening heart-connection with his parents was a pivotal part of John's decision to put his full faith and trust in Christ for the forgiveness of his sins.

It is now ten years later. John meets weekly with his parents for a time of family worship. They read the Bible together, share what God is doing in their lives, and pray for one another. John concluded our interview with this: "If I ever have a family, I'm so excited that I have my parents to be my children's grandparents. I look forward to sharing life with them, taking a deep interest in each other's lives, and having them spiritually influence my children. It's such a blessing to have the kind of relationship where we really know each other, and where we encourage and pray for each other in everything."

Remember four biblical principles that God gives to parents?

- Offer your heart to the Lord.
- Turn your heart to your child.
- Draw your child's heart to yours.
- Point your child's heart to Christ.

In the real-life story above, John's parents were excellent examples of the second principle. Their hearts were turned toward their son. Despite his rebellion, their hearts did not harden toward him, but they continued to extend warmth and a desire for him to return to them and to the Lord.

The first two parenting principles—offering our hearts to the Lord, and turning our hearts to our children—are personal and internal. The convictions and actions that go with them take place in the privacy of our hearts. But don't rush past them. They lay the spiritual foundation for the action plan to come. God often needs to do dramatic work in our spirits prior to calling us to new levels of impact in the lives of others.

TURNING HEARTS—THE BRIDGE BETWEEN
THE TESTAMENTS

The biblical principle of parents turning their hearts to their children comes to us from the last paragraph of the last book of the Old Testament.

Last words are important. I sat beside my father on his deathbed, pen and paper in hand, and wrote down many things that he said to me. It was a once-in-a-lifetime moment, and I gave my full attention to his every word. God chose to end the Old Testament era of divine revelation with these last words:

> Remember the law of my servant Moses, the decrees and laws I gave him at Horeb for all Israel. See, I will send you the prophet Elijah before that great and dreadful day of the LORD comes. He will turn the hearts of the fathers to their children, and the hearts of the children to their fathers; or else I will come and strike the land with a curse. (Mal. 4:4–6)

God says that the day is coming when fathers are going to turn their hearts to their children, and their children are going to respond by turning their hearts back to their fathers. The hearts of fathers and children will be united in the Lord. But then we find a warning. If this does not happen, God's desired plan of blessing His people will be broken. Instead of a blessing, there will be a curse. The text specifically speaks to the ministry of fathers, and how vital it is that the hearts of fathers be turned toward their children. God is not ignoring the influence of a faithful mother, but this text stresses the power of a faithful father, a father whose heart is turned and focused on the souls of his children.

It would be over four hundred years before God would once again give more written revelation to His people in the New Testament. And God's desire for the hearts of parents, particularly fathers, to be turned to their children serves as the beginning of the New Testament as well. The heart-connection between parents and children is the bridge between the testaments.[1] If you were to make a movie of the events of the New Testament, what would be the first scene? Do you remember the first thing that happens in the story of Jesus? The events leading up to the coming of Messiah begin when God sends the angel Gabriel to speak to a man named Zechariah. Zechariah was married to Elizabeth, and they were unable to have children. Gabriel's words to Zechariah serve as the first words of revelation in the New Testament. Four hundred years earlier, God had spoken through Malachi that He desired the hearts of fathers to be turned to their children. Now the angel Gabriel speaks to Zechariah and tells him about a son who will soon be born to him:

> *God says that the day is coming when fathers are going to turn their hearts to their children, and their children are going to respond by turning their hearts back to their fathers.*

> Many of the people of Israel will he bring back to the Lord their God. And he will go on before the Lord, in the spirit and power of Elijah, to turn the hearts of the fathers to their children and the disobedient to the wisdom of the righteous—to make ready a people prepared for the Lord. (Luke 1:16–17)

We know Zechariah's son as John the Baptist. When we think of John we understand that God sent him to prepare the way for Jesus. But what was his strategy? How would John seek to get the people ready for the Christ? Gabriel tells us that John would "*turn the hearts of the fathers to their children* and the disobedient to the wisdom of the righteous—to make ready a people prepared for the Lord" (emphasis added). Central to John's mission to prepare the hearts of people for Messiah was to turn the hearts of fathers to their children. Why? Because when fathers turn their hearts to their children, the hearts of children are softened to receive the love of God.

You're reading this book because you want to see the heart of your son or daughter prepared for Jesus. You want your child to receive Christ in faith and to love Him with all his or her heart. So what can you do to encourage your child to turn to God? You can turn your heart to your child. You can ask God to fill your heart with focus, compassion, and a compelling drive to do all in your power to help your children get safely home to their Father in heaven.

ORDERING OUR HEARTS

Earlier, I shared with you how God turned my heart to my children after I'd spent many years having my heart at work. My dreams and passions centered on my ministry and impact at church, but I was neglecting my primary calling, which is the spiritual leadership of my wife and children. I had quietly believed a lie of the world, that my meaning and purpose were to be found primarily in my ministry outside my home, rather than in my ministry to my family. Satan loves to take God's order for our lives and turn it upside down and inside out. Consider the following diagram that depicts the proper order of our loves.

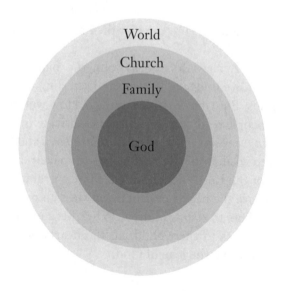

God wants our loves to be ordered. He wants our love for Him to be at the center of our lives. He wants us to love Him above all others. Jesus points us to the book of Deuteronomy, where we find the first and greatest commandment: "Love the LORD your God with all your heart and with all your soul and with all your strength" (6:5).

Next in the order of our loves, Scripture calls us to love the members of our family. Ministry begins with family. Calling and purpose begin at home. In the Ten Commandments, found in Exodus 20, the first four commandments are vertical—they have to do with our relationship with God. The last six commandments are horizontal—they instruct us as to God's will for our human relationships. The fifth commandment, which is the first commandment in the list that focuses on human relationships, is "Honor your father and your mother" (v. 12).

God Himself wrote the commandments into the stone tablets. He arranged the commandments in a specific order. He wrote the command to honor our parents before the commands not to murder or commit adultery. This is not to minimize the seriousness of these other sins, but rather to show us that the first issue that children must address in their lives is how they will relate to their parents. Will they honor and obey them, or will they dishonor and rebel against them? This is life's first hurdle.

Within the love for family, husbands are called to love their wives with a supernatural and top-priority love. God speaks to husbands through the apostle Paul: "Husbands, love your wives, just as Christ loved the church and gave himself up for her" (Eph. 5:25). Could there be a stronger love than this? God desires that a husband love his wife more than any other person. If a husband's love for another is greater than his love for his wife, his heart is not, in fact, ordered rightly.

When it comes to generosity, meeting the needs of others, and caring for the poor, God is clear—family is to come first. In the book of 1 Timothy, Paul gives instructions to the church on how to care for the poor. He writes, "If anyone does not provide for his relatives, and especially for his immediate family, he has denied the faith and is worse than an unbeliever" (5:8). If a Christian is generous with his church family, but stingy with his own family, his heart is not ordered rightly.

This is not to say that our relationships at church are not important. Our relationships with our brothers and sisters in Christ should, in fact, come in our next circle of priority: love for God first, then love for family, then love for spiritual family. Jesus taught that being in right relationships with our brothers and sisters in Christ was a prerequisite for effective ministry and evangelism in the community.

When it comes to generosity, meeting the needs of others, and caring for the poor, God is clear—family is to come first.

He taught his disciples, "By this all men will know that you are my disciples, if you love one another" (John 13:35). If we are not committed to practicing Christian love in our church family, why would anyone ever want to join our church family? People in the church should be under no illusion that they can successfully minister to the community without seeking first to be in right relationships with one another.

The fourth circle, the outer circle, is our ministry to the world. This takes place in our neighborhoods, at our workplaces and schools, on the mission field, and elsewhere.

I have a deep concern that in many churches today, we fail to teach God's Word in regard to the ordering of our loves. In many churches it seems that the message, week after week, is "Get right with God, and go make a difference in the world!" Circle 1... Circle 4... Week after week. I believe that if we do not embrace a radical commitment to a biblical ordering of our loves and lives—God, family, church, world—then we will continue to see a dramatic decline of Christian faith in our culture.

The joyous Christian life is built from the inside out. It is built upon a right ordering of hearts, loves, and lives. The more we ask God to order our hearts properly, the more our families and churches are prepared for transformational ministry that will impact our communities and the world.

If God desires our hearts to be ordered in this way, we should expect the enemy to do all in his power to twist and pervert this order. Satan's strategy is not surprising. Where is the last place that Satan wants our hearts? You can answer the question by asking where is the first place God wants our hearts? God wants our first love with Him, so that's where Satan focuses his first attacks. The enemy doesn't mind if you go through the Christian motions. He can tolerate you going to church, giving your tithe, and going to your Bible study... as long as you don't love God with all your heart, with all your soul, and with all your strength.

What is the enemy's next priority, after doing all he can to take your heart away from Christ? His next attack will be to take your heart away from your family. He'll do everything he can to break the heart-connection between husbands and wives, parents and children, siblings, grandparents and grandchildren.

One of his top priorities is to break the heart-connection between you and your children. Here again, he doesn't mind if you go through the motions, paying the bills, trying to be a nice person, and spending time together as a family... as long as you don't cross the line of turning your family into a discipleship center, a worship center, a service center, and an evangelism center. Satan doesn't care if your family enjoys being together and if you get along well; his concern is that your family does not engage with each other spiritually.

You will also find spiritual resistance in the third priority circle. The enemy loves to stir up conflict, gossip, and dissension in the local church. Churches that are filled with bitterness and infighting are effectively neutralized.

Our secular modern culture, which is influenced by the forces of evil, seeks to completely reverse the heart-order that God desires for us. God created us so that our hearts would be first with Him, then our families, then our church families. From that foundation of love and community, our families and churches would reach the world for Christ. The culture calls us to the exact opposite: Your first love should be the world! Your job, your hobbies, your dreams, your ambitions, and your stuff should occupy the first place in your heart. If you want to do the church thing, that's okay, as long as you don't overdo it. Family is fine but that's not where you're going to find real meaning. And God? Well, that old-fashioned idea is little more than a psychological crutch. You don't really need a crutch, do you?

Every one of us must choose how we will order our loves. God pleads with us in the Scriptures not to put the world first in our hearts:

> If you belonged to the world, it would love you as its own. As it is, you do not belong to the world, but I have chosen you out of the world. That is why the world hates you. (John 15:19)

> Do not love the world or anything in the world. If anyone loves the world, the love of the Father is not in him. (1 John 2:15)

For so many years, my heart was in the outer two circles. My passion, drive, dreams, and focus were on my ministry at church and in the community. It was not wrong to love and be committed to those things, but it was sinful for my loves to be out of order. I was a hollow Christian man. When people looked at me, they saw the outer circles. They saw my ministry at church, and some were impressed. I got a lot of affirmation and encouragement. But I was a shell of a man. The outer circles were thriving, but I wasn't right with my children, my wife, and my Lord. My secondary calling at church and in the community was in high gear, while my primary calling, my ministry at home, was suffering.

I was deeply convicted by reading Billy Graham's autobiography, *Just As I Am*. In the last chapter, he talks about things he would have done differently:

> Ruth says those of us who were off traveling missed the best part of our lives—enjoying the children as they grew. She is

probably right. I was too busy preaching all over the world....
I now know that I came through those years much the poorer
both psychologically and emotionally. I missed so much by
not being home to see the children grow and develop. The
children must carry the scars of those separations too....

I have failed many times, and I would do many things
differently. For one thing, I would speak less and study more,
and I would spend more time with my family. When I look
back over the schedule I kept thirty or forty years ago, I am
staggered by all the things we did and the engagements we
kept. Sometimes we flitted from one part of the country to
another, even from one continent to another, in the course
of only a few days. Were all those engagements necessary?...
Every day I was absent from my family is gone forever. [2]

I wonder what *I* would do if someone asked me to spend a
year traveling the world, preaching the gospel at the great sta-
diums? I'm pretty confident I'll never have to wrestle with that
decision, but what *would* I do? Unless I could take my family, I
believe I would say no. God has spoken clearly to me in the Bible
about the mission of my life. He has instructed me in Ephesians
6:4, "Fathers, do not exasperate your children; instead, bring
them up in the training and instruction of the Lord." Any ministry opportunity that would prevent me from being obedient to
that command would have to be delayed or declined. I could not
be an obedient Christian man, and at the same time neglect the
spiritual training of my children while they're in my home. God
would need either to make a way for my family to be with me,
or He would have to bring that opportunity to me later in life.

Over the past five years, God has turned my heart to my children. By His grace, I now find my greatest desire to nurture faith
in them. That turning has been an answer to prayer. I regularly
pray, in fact, for God to turn my heart to Him, then to my wife,
then to my children, then to my church. I pray that from a right
ordering of my heart and life, God would use my family and my
church to show His glory to the world.

Two years ago, I experienced something I'd never experienced before. You may find this hard to believe. I was sitting at my desk at church in the middle of the afternoon. The day was going along just fine, and I'd just finished a project and was transitioning to something else. In that brief moment of down time, I had a thought that I'd never had before. *I'm really looking forward to going home and being with my family.* "What?" you ask. "You had never had that thought before?" No. Not while I was at work. When at work, I thought about work. (And in those days, when I was at *home* I thought about work.) That thought, though, was an indication to me that God was answering my prayers. He was turning my heart to my family. He was rightly ordering my loves.

I encourage you to start praying this same prayer. Start right now. Turn your attention to the Lord in prayer. Ask Him plainly and simply, "God, I want my heart to be rightly ordered. I live in a world that bombards me every day to take my heart away from You, from my family, and from my church. I need You to order my loves. I need You to turn my heart first toward You, then toward my family. Specifically, please turn my heart to my children. By Your grace, I ask that You help me see my role in my family, particularly my calling as a parent, as my most important ministry in the world."

A HEART OF COMPASSION

When our hearts are turned to our children, particularly our children who are far from God, the Lord increasingly gives us a spirit of compassion toward them. In the book of Matthew, we find a beautiful picture of Christ's heart for the lost: "When he saw the crowds, he had compassion on them, because they were harassed and helpless, like sheep without a shepherd" (9:36). Is this how you see your children who are far from the Lord? Do you have a child who has not trusted Christ as the Lord and Savior of his or her life? Jesus looked at the lost and He saw them as harassed, helpless... like sheep without a shepherd. It's hard for us to admit it, but it's very easy for a judgmental and critical spirit to arise in us, even toward our own children. If it's your desire to turn your heart to your child, you must also pray earnestly for God to give you His heart for your son or daughter.

I've spent countless hours with young adults who have rejected Christ and the Christian life. Not one of these young people, in my judgment, rejected Christ on purely intellectual grounds. Some of them told me that was the reason. They talked about their biology class in the public school where they became convinced that evolution was true, or their college philosophy class where they learned that truth depends on one's perspective. Indeed, those deceptive worldviews impacted their walk with God. However, in every situation that I've heard those things, further conversations have revealed deeper reasons... hurt, pain, rejection, abandonment, sin, rebellion, abuse. The list could go on. Their hearts experienced a mixture of sin and wounding that drove them far from God.

It's very easy for a judgmental and critical spirit to arise in us, even toward our own children.

Have no doubt that your child is in a spiritual battle. At the moment, the enemy is thrilled to have the upper hand in the heart of your child. He has no plan to let up. He will continue to pummel your child with deceptions, pain, trauma, rejection, and temptation. He has your son or daughter down, and he wants nothing more than to keep your child down. He will do all he can to keep your child's heart far from you, far from church, far from the Scriptures, and far from Jesus. Your son or daughter is under direct assault from the forces of evil and from our evil culture.

My point is not to make excuses for our children, but to face the reality that they are under horrible spiritual attack, and that should drive us to our knees and fill us with an overwhelming compassion for them. Your son is being harassed. Your daughter is like a sheep without a shepherd. If you're going to embrace the mission to do all in your power to lead your child to Christ, you must ask God to fill your heart with compassion. No matter what your son or daughter says, every human being wants love, understanding, and compassion.

LOVE ME

"Love Me" is the title of one of my favorite songs, performed by J. J. Heller. I believe these words echo in the hearts of our prodigal children.

> He cries in the corner where nobody sees.
> He's the kid with the story no one would believe.
> He prays every night, "Dear God won't you please,
> Could you send someone here who will love me?"

> Who will love me for me?
> Not for what I have done or what I will become.
> Who will love me for me?
> 'Cause nobody has shown me what love, what love really
>   means.

> Her office is shrinking a little each day.
> She's the woman whose husband has run away.
> She'll go to the gym after working today.
> Maybe if she was thinner
> Then he would've stayed.
> And she says...

> Who will love me for me?
> Not for what I have done or what I will become.
> Who will love me for me?
> 'Cause nobody has shown me what love, what love really
>   means.

> He's waiting to die as he sits all alone.
> He's a man in a cell who regrets what he's done.
> He utters a cry from the depths of his soul,
> "Oh Lord, forgive me, I want to go home."

Then he heard a voice somewhere deep inside,
And it said,
"I know you've murdered and I know you've lied.
I have watched you suffer all of your life,
And now that you'll listen, I'll tell you that I..."

I will love you for you.
Not for what you have done or what you will become.
I will love you for you.
I will give you the love,
The love that you never knew.[3]

Before we continue our journey in the next chapter, take another moment to pray. Ask the Lord, "Please fill my heart with Your compassion for my child. Never let me forget the intense spiritual attack that _____ is going through. Help me to see my child through Your eyes."

Questions for Reflection/Discussion

1. Why do you think God places such a high priority on the hearts of parents being turned to their children, and the hearts of children being turned to their parents?
2. Consider the four circles/priorities of the Christian life. In what ways do you struggle keeping these in the right order?
3. In what ways has your child cried out, "Who will love me for me?"

Chapter 6

THE FREEDOM OF FORGIVENESS

IN THE PREVIOUS CHAPTER we talked about the biblical principle of turning our hearts to our children. We now need to talk about a deep and potentially dangerous barrier in our journey to encourage faith in our sons and daughters. We don't like to admit it, but it's easy for bitterness, resentment, and unforgiveness to creep into our hearts—even toward our own children.

Many of you have experienced deep wounds because of the words your children have spoken and the choices your children have made. When I was a kid, in a fit of anger, I told my mother that I hated her. I believe I only said it once. I apologized and she forgave me. Many parents have heard those horrible words hundreds of times from their children, and their hurt turned to bitterness, and their bitterness finally turned to anger. The closer people are to us, the more power they have to hurt us. God has built a deep and irrevocable connection between our hearts and the hearts of our children. No one can compete with our power as parents to damage the hearts of our children. But hurt is a two-way street. With a look or a subtle tone of voice, our children can wound us like no one else.

Perhaps your child has brought public shame on your family and you haven't been able to shake your feelings of resentment. Maybe the years of disrespect and snide remarks have caused your heart to be numb at best and bitter at worst. Have your children ridiculed you because of your faith in Christ? Few things hurt more than when our own children declare that they don't believe in the God of the Bible.

These hurts can accumulate and escalate to such a tragic degree that relationships become virtually nonexistent, with years passing between even the briefest moments of contact. You may find yourself in the heartbreaking situation where your children will not answer the phone or respond to e-mail. They've made the choice to shut you out of their lives. But sometimes parents are the ones who shut out their children by withdrawing from them, sometimes even excommunicating them from the family. Love requires appropriate boundaries, but never gives up on the hope and desire for reconciliation. If your child has deeply hurt you, Satan desires to fill your heart with anger to such a degree that you'll be incapable of feeling compassion.

Unless we're able to forgive our children for the ways they've hurt us, we won't be free to love them and pursue them with truth and grace.

Unforgiveness is a devastating barrier to our mission to encourage faith in the hearts of our children. Unless we're able to forgive our children for the ways they've hurt us, we won't be free to love them and pursue them with truth and grace. Unfortunately, it's easy to find pat answers about what forgiveness is and how it works. In this chapter, we'll explore God's Word to discover the path of true forgiveness—and the freedom it brings.

MY STORY

The greatest hurt I ever experienced was from my father. When my parents got married, neither of them had trusted Christ as Lord and Savior of their lives. By God's grace, my mother put her full faith and trust in Christ when I was three months old. Her life was transformed, and she did all she could to impress my heart with a love for God. My father's heart was cold toward spiritual things, and their marriage became increasingly strained. My parents divorced when I was a sophomore in high school. It was an awful time, filled with pain and confusion. The divorce, selling our home, moving to a new high school—it was all terribly difficult to face.

But that was not the worst of it. The trigger for my parents' divorce was the discovery that my father had been involved with other women. For me, a boy growing into manhood, his behavior was devastating. How could he do this to Mom? How could he do this to our family? How could he do this to me?

I know that many of you have experienced hurts far more serious than this. But I've never experienced a deeper wound. I began to descend into the pit of unforgiveness. Hurt began to take Satan's desired path to resentment, resentment to bitterness, bitterness to rage, and rage to hatred.

BITTER ROOTS

God warns us about bitterness in the book of Hebrews, and I was beginning to experience it: "See to it that no one misses the grace of God and that no bitter root grows up to cause trouble and defile many" (12:15). In this Scripture, God teaches how bitterness grows, using an analogy of how plants grow. When someone does something to hurt us, those hurts are like seeds of bitterness seeking to plant themselves in our hearts. If we ignore those seeds, or water them, more bitterness will grow. It will sprout roots. Eventually, the bitterness in our hearts will grow up to cause trouble not only for us, but it will defile others as well.

The Albizia falcata, found in Malaysia, is believed to be the fastest growing tree in the world. When the seeds of this tree are planted, nothing sprouts for a whole year. Five years go by, in fact, without any sign of life. At the end of the fifth year, a shoot appears... and the tree can grow thirty-five feet in one year![1] They say that you can hear it cracking as it grows. What was happening for those five years? Above the surface, nothing was visible, but below the surface, roots were growing hundreds of feet in all directions. The tree was gathering nutrients and strength for its eventual burst upward.

This is a picture of Hebrews 12:15. Unforgiveness works just like this seed. As soon as it is planted, the growth process begins. When our family members hurt us, seeds of bitterness are often planted deep in the soil of our hearts. The seed will go to work, building a root system, preparing for a day in the future. Then suddenly bitterness will shoot forth into our lives, causing trouble and defiling many. We fail to recognize that some of the trouble in our lives and in our relationships is actually the fruit born of seeds of bitterness planted long ago... seeds that were fed with time and neglect. Unforgiveness and joy cannot live together in the human heart. If Satan has his way, bitterness will master us and spread to those around us.

THE GIFT OF FORGIVENESS

Every family is filled with hurt. It's impossible to be close to other sinful human beings without them hurting us. We've hurt our children, and they've hurt us. Is there any hope to escape the tangled branches of bitterness and unforgiveness? Consider God's words as written through the apostle Paul:

> Therefore, as God's chosen people, holy and dearly loved, clothe yourselves with compassion, kindness, humility, gentleness and patience. Bear with each other and forgive whatever grievances you may have against one another. Forgive as the Lord forgave you. And over all these virtues put on love, which binds them all together in perfect unity. (Col. 3:12–14)

The path of freedom begins with a command from God— "Forgive as the Lord forgave you." Why would God tell us to do this? He calls us to forgive because He loves us, and He knows what bitterness and unforgiveness do to us. They destroy us from the inside out. Unforgiveness is like a disease that hardens our hearts. Bitterness may seem like a weapon we can use to protect ourselves from being hurt again, but as we wield it, we're the ones who are wounded. Anger is like a grenade that we want to use to hurt those who've hurt us. But when we pull the pin to heave it, it sticks to our hand... and we pay the price. *Forgive as the Lord forgave you.* God does not ask us to do something that He hasn't already done Himself. Imagine a set of scales. On the right side, pile up all the things that you've done to offend God—all the sins you've committed. On the left side, pile up all of the things that your son or daughter has done to offend you—all the sins your child committed to cause you pain. Look at the piles. Which way do the scales tip? No contest! Our sins against God—both sins of commission and omission—are beyond measurement or comprehension. Yet, despite our lifetime of sin against the Creator, what has He done? "God demonstrates his own love for us in this: While we were still sinners, Christ died for us" (Rom. 5:8). "For God so loved the world that he gave his one and only Son, that whoever believes in him shall not perish but have eternal life" (John 3:16).

God chose to offer forgiveness for all of our sins—and at the greatest of personal costs to Himself. God then calls His people to follow in His footsteps—*Forgive as the Lord forgave you.* Choose forgiveness, even if it costs you greatly. We can choose forgiveness or remain in bondage to bitterness. There are only two paths available.

FREELY RECEIVE, FREELY GIVE

Christians love to talk about the great gift of God's grace and forgiveness. We're grateful for Jesus, who took all our sins upon Himself on the cross and who died in our place. Christ's death and resurrection make it possible for us to be forgiven of all our sins—past, present, and future—yet we struggle when it comes to forgiving our family members who have hurt us. Jesus confronts each of us through one of His parables: "Therefore, the kingdom of heaven is like a king who wanted to settle accounts with his servants. As he began the settlement, a man who owed him ten thousand talents was brought to him" (Matt. 18:23–24). How much money is ten thousand talents? When David built the magnificent temple to the Lord it cost three thousand talents. Jesus' point is that this debt is astronomical. The story continues:

> Since he was not able to pay, the master ordered that he and his wife and his children and all that he had be sold to repay the debt.
>
> The servant fell on his knees before him. "Be patient with me," he begged, "and I will pay back everything." The servant's master took pity on him, canceled the debt and let him go.
>
> But when that servant went out, he found one of his fellow servants who owed him a hundred denarii [an amount that would be less than a hundred dollars]. He grabbed him and began to choke him. "Pay back what you owe me!" he demanded.
>
> His fellow servant fell to his knees and begged him, "Be patient with me, and I will pay you back."
>
> But he refused. Instead, he went off and had the man thrown into prison until he could pay the debt. When the other servants saw what had happened, they were greatly distressed and went and told their master everything that had happened.
>
> Then the master called the servant in. "You wicked servant," he said, "I canceled all that debt of yours because you begged me to. Shouldn't you have had mercy on your fellow servant just as I had on you?" In anger his master turned him over to the jailers to be tortured, until he should pay back all he owed.
>
> This is how my heavenly Father will treat each of you unless you forgive your brother from your heart. (Matt. 18:25–35)

God takes forgiveness very seriously—both His work of forgiveness for us, and His command for us to forgive others. In no uncertain terms, Jesus tells us that if we, after receiving the merciful forgiveness of God, fail to forgive those who have offended us, pain and torment are not far behind. We will be imprisoned in our own bitterness, and even our relationship with God will suffer. If we desire to turn our hearts toward our children, we need to commit ourselves to forgiving them for the things they've done to hurt us.

FORGIVENESS MYTHS

In a few moments we'll look carefully at a biblical forgiveness path, but first we need to clear up some common misconceptions. When it comes to forgiveness, we hear a lot of pat answers as well as myths. One common myth is that forgiving someone means trusting that person again. If your son has stolen money from the family, forgiving him does not mean trusting him again with access to family resources. That would be foolish. Parents should respond to such a sin in two ways. First, the parents should forgive their son. They should go to God and tell Him how much their son's sin has hurt them, and that they choose to forgive him. They choose to forgive him, as the Lord has forgiven them. They should then pray and ask God to guard their hearts from any hatred, bitterness, or resentment. Second, the parents should not fully trust their son for the foreseeable future. His choice to steal must be met with natural consequences. He should no longer have access to family resources and should not be fully trusted in financial and, perhaps, other matters. The parents can fully and totally forgive their son for stealing from them—setting their hearts free from hatred and bitterness—while at the same time withdrawing trust from him until it's earned back again. Forgiving does not mean trusting.

A second myth is that forgiving means restoring warm feelings toward the offender. Some people think that if they forgive, that means they need to "like" the people who committed offenses against them. This is ridiculous. If your daughter is consistently rude to you, it's not realistic to expect that you'll have warm feelings toward her. We have warm feelings toward those who are nice to us, plain and simple. Why do you think that God never commands us in the Bible to "like" people? Rather, we're commanded to love—regardless of whether or not we feel warm toward the offender. Many parents tell me, "I just can't seem to forgive my daughter for the things she's done... and continues to do. I try and try, but I still don't feel affection for her." They're getting forgiveness mixed up with warm feelings. It's possible to completely forgive your daughter and to be free from bitterness and hatred, but still not have a feeling of warm affection for her.

If you're waiting until you feel like forgiving your child, you may be waiting the rest of your life.

I believe that our confusion between forgiveness and feelings often prevents us from following the biblical path to freedom. Here, a third myth can creep in; time heals all wounds. This is one of Satan's subtle lies. Time is exactly what seeds of hurt and bitterness need in order to grow. When it comes to dealing with the things our children have done to hurt us, time is not on our side. The sooner we face those hurts and commit ourselves to a biblical forgiveness process, the sooner we'll find the freedom that God desires for us.

A fourth myth is, forgiving means forgetting. While we're called to be godly, we are not God. We cannot cast someone's sin "as far as the east is from the west" (Ps. 103:12). That is a divine ability, not a human one. If a person has deeply hurt you, you cannot erase what happened from your memory banks. I've talked with many believers who are racked with guilt because they can't seem to forget what others have done to them and so they think they haven't forgiven the offenders. When we forgive those who have hurt us, we don't minimize the seriousness of what happened, nor will we completely forget it. Rather, the seriousness of our hurt and our painful memories are overshadowed by the supernatural grace of God. Our memories may not be erased, but we can be free.

THREE PHASES OF BIBLICAL FORGIVENESS

Forgiveness with the Will

Biblical forgiveness has three phases. The first step of true forgiveness is a choice. It is an act of the will. If God commands us to forgive, then we have a choice whether or not we will obey. This first step—forgiveness with the will—has nothing to do with our feelings. Many parents say that they'll be ready to forgive when...

- my son apologizes for what he did.
- my daughter starts making better choices.
- I sense a changed attitude in my child. • more time passes and I've had more time to "process."

If you're waiting until you *feel* like forgiving your child, you may be waiting the rest of your life. Forgiving is not something that comes naturally to us. It forces us to become vulnerable and submit ourselves to Christ. I invite you to begin an intentional forgiveness process even now. A genuine forgiveness process begins with prayer. I encourage you to quiet your heart now and pray:

> Lord, I want to be free of any bitterness, resentment, and anger I may have in my heart toward _____. I want to be free to love my child, pursue my child, and do all I can to point my child's heart toward Christ. I can't afford to have any bitterness stand in the way. Please bring to my mind now all the things that _____ has done to hurt me. Please show me anything in our past that I need to forgive.

Write down what the Lord brings to mind. Start with the line, "It hurt me when _____ (your child's name)..." Be as specific as you can. Identify events, words, actions, and attitudes. This first step of *forgiveness with the will* can be a painful one. No one likes to bring up and relive memories like these. But remember the lie we identified earlier—time does not heal all wounds. Time allows wounds to fester, become infected, and eventually destroy us.

When I had to take this step of forgiveness with my father, I wrote down things like this:

- It hurt me when my father cheated on the family.
- It hurt me when Dad told me he did not believe in Jesus.
- It hurt me when Dad would not go to marriage counseling.

If you've written some things down, the time has come to obey the Scriptures, grit your teeth, and choose to forgive your child for the things he or she has done to hurt you. Put your feelings aside. Now is the time to "forgive as the Lord forgave you" (Col. 3:13).

When it came to this moment in my journey with my father, everything in me did not want to do this! My father didn't deserve forgiveness, and I didn't want to grant it. But God gave me the strength to pray. I looked at my list and I prayed out loud, "God, I don't feel like forgiving my father. I don't feel he deserves it. Despite my feelings, I choose to be obedient to You right now. I choose to forgive Dad for cheating on the family. I choose to forgive him for not believing in you. I choose to forgive him for not going to marriage counseling..." Line after line, I worked my way down the list. "I choose to forgive... I choose to forgive..."

I encourage you to take the first step of forgiveness now. If you wrote down any words, actions, events, or attitudes from your son or daughter that have hurt you, make the choice to forgive your child now. Pray out loud. A whisper will do. "God, I choose to obey your command to forgive _____ for the things that have been done to hurt me. I choose to forgive my child for..." Pain by pain, hurt by hurt, choose to forgive.

Forgiveness with the Heart
The first phase of biblical forgiveness is forgiveness with the will. That phase can be done in fifteen minutes, but it can take

decades to get to the point of making the choice to do it. I pray that you have just taken this all-important step of obedience. If you did, you are on a new path to freedom in your relationship with your child. Once we have chosen to forgive our sons and daughters for the things they've done to hurt us, we enter the second phase of forgiveness—forgiveness with the heart.

Jesus ends the parable of the unmerciful servant with these words; "forgive your brother from your heart" (Matt. 18:35). Up until now, we've been talking about the need to put our feelings aside. In this second phase, we turn to God and ask Him to set us free from our resentment, bitterness, and anger. Only God has the power to change our hearts and our feelings. If you struggle with bitterness toward your child, I'm confident that you've never made an active choice to *be* bitter toward your son or daughter. You've never awakened in the morning and said, "I'm going to do everything I can today to foster an attitude of bitterness toward my child!" You haven't used willpower to "put on" these feelings, and willpower will not cast them off. We are now dealing with matters of the heart, and therefore we need to turn to God—the only one with the power to change our hearts.

When it came to my feelings about my father, I was like a bucket filled with mud and sludge. The years had dripped hurt and pain into my life to the point that I was full and overflowing. When I chose to forgive him, it was like taking a hammer and smashing a hole in the bottom of the bucket. It was a declaration that I wanted to be free from the curse of bitterness. But if you hammer a hole into the bottom of a sludge bucket, the sludge doesn't come out all at once. It oozes out, one ugly glop at a time. The second phase of forgiveness is the process by which God drains our hearts of our bitterness, resentment, and hatred.

Do you want to forgive your son or daughter from your heart? Do you want to be free from resentment? I encourage you to begin the next phase of forgiveness with this prayer:

God, I have chosen to be obedient to You, and to forgive _____ for the things that have been done to hurt me.

But I am powerless over the dark feelings in my heart. I cannot heal my own heart of bitterness, resentment, and anger. Only You can do that. I give You permission, and I ask You in faith to heal my heart. Help me forgive my child from my heart. Work on me for as long as it takes to free my heart from any and all unforgiveness.

This second phase of forgiveness can last a long time. I prayed like this for more than four years, continually asking the Lord to do what I could not do... heal my heart toward my father. One day, as a junior in college, I was getting ready to leave my apartment and my thoughts drifted to my father. I was immediately struck by the feeling in my heart toward him. Compassion! The sludge bucket had been drained.

Over those four years, God had healed my heart of my hatred for my father. I now could see him as harassed and helpless, like a sheep without a shepherd, and my heart went out to him like never before. I began to think often of how his life was affected by his mother's death in the hospital just days after she gave birth to him. He was adopted by an unmarried uncle who told him repeatedly that Jesus was just a man. My dad never had a godly male role model. He spent his life looking for love and acceptance. My mother was his fourth wife. Yes, he committed terrible sins. Yes, he caused the breakup of my family. When we forgive someone, we don't minimize the seriousness of what has happened. Instead, the seriousness of the hurt is overshadowed by the supernatural grace of God. I had become free to pursue a new relationship with my father, and do all in my power to point his heart toward Jesus—the One who could give him the love he was looking for.

I hope you have decided to enter this second phase of forgiveness by earnestly asking God to heal your heart. No one can tell you how long God will take to complete this process, so you must continually bring this prayer to Him, trusting Him to set you free in His time.

Reconciliation

As we've seen, the first phase of biblical forgiveness is *forgiveness with the will*. The second phase is *forgiveness with the heart*. The third phase is *reconciliation*. This is the marvelous culmination when your relationship with your son or daughter is healed and restored. It's essential for us to understand that each of these phases requires a primary agent. Who is primarily responsible for the first phase, forgiveness with the will? Who must act if it is to happen? We must. We must choose obedience, and choose to forgive. If we don't make that choice, forgiveness cannot happen.

Who is primarily responsible for the second phase, forgiveness with the heart? Who must act if it is to happen? God. God must act and avail His power on our behalf to free our hearts of bitterness and resentment. If He does not act, it will not happen.

Consider now this third phase—reconciliation. It also requires a primary agent. Who must act for reconciliation to take place? Sometimes we think that the primary burden for reconciliation lies with us, but that is not the case. Consider my journey with my father. By God's grace, He led me through the first two phases of forgiveness. My heart was set free from anger and resentment. I then went to my father and I told him that I'd forgiven him for what he'd done. The conversation was cordial, but his response was not heartfelt.

Reconciliation cannot happen without repentance.

Is it wrong to tell someone that you've forgiven him or her? No, but announcing your choice to forgive does not create reconciliation. Reconciliation cannot happen without repentance. Forgiveness is a gift, which must be requested. It cannot be forced on your children, just as you can't force them to open a special Christmas present.

Who is the primary agent of reconciliation? Who must act for reconciliation to take place? Your son or daughter must eventually repent, express sorrow over what he or she did, and ask for your forgiveness. Please don't hear me saying, "This is all your child's fault!" It's likely that you've both done things that have hurt each other, and that repentance is required on both sides before reconciliation can happen.

Reconciliation, however, may never happen. You can't control what your son or daughter will choose to do. I couldn't control what my father would choose to do. Everything in me wanted him to repent and ask my forgiveness. I'd already forgiven him. The gift of forgiveness was wrapped with a big bow on top, just waiting for him to ask for it. I was eager, even desperate, to reconcile with my father, and more importantly, to see him reconciled to God.

On August 10, in a hospital bed, my father, Bill, made the decision to put his full faith and trust in Christ for the forgiveness of his sins. He repented and was reconciled to God. Through God's grace and providence, my mother, Angie (his fourth wife), and her husband, Jack (my stepfather), had the honor of praying with him to accept Christ. My father's repentance, conversion, and salvation is the greatest miracle I have ever seen in my life.[2]

Shortly after my father's repentance, my family and I jumped into the car and drove halfway across the country to see him... for one last time. We arrived on August 16, my birthday. I went immediately to see my father in the care center, and we shared the best ninety minutes of our lives together. He was a changed man. The old was gone, and the new had come.

On September 3, 2008, my father died. He was ninety years old. I'd been praying most of my life to be reconciled with my father and to see him reconciled to God. God had answered.

There are no guarantees what will happen in your relationship with your son or daughter. We don't know if your child will ever repent and seek forgiveness from you and from God. But you must radically commit yourself to forgiving your son or daughter with your will and then from your heart—so that if and when your child turns his or her heart to you, you'll be ready. The gift of forgiveness will be wrapped and prepared for your son or daughter... all he or she will need to do is ask.

I've seen tragedy occur, though, many times. Children come to their parents, humbly seeking forgiveness, and because the parents had not been obedient to God and chosen to forgive their children, the parents were unwilling to forgive. The children were sent away empty-handed. How God's heart must break in moments like those! *Forgive as the Lord forgave you.*

Questions for Reflection/Discussion

1. When you were growing up, how did your family deal with hurt feelings and broken relationships?
2. In the past, how have you handled unwanted negative feelings toward your child?
3. Do you need to take active steps in the forgiveness process? If yes, when can you set aside time to do it?

Chapter 7

DRAW YOUR CHILD'S HEART TO YOURS

WE'VE JOURNEYED THROUGH THE first two biblical principles of building a heart-connection to our children—offering our hearts to the Lord, and turning our hearts to our children. The work up until this point has been underground. We've been digging into and then laying a spiritual foundation in our own hearts in order to prepare for action. In order to pursue the goal, we need to do all in our power to be right with God and to be free to love our children. Do you remember the goal that we talked about earlier?

- Your son, loving God with all his heart, putting his full faith and trust in Jesus for his present and his future, and arriving safely home in heaven together.
- Your daughter, loving God with all her heart, putting her full faith and trust in Jesus for her present and her future, and arriving safely home in heaven together.

Take a moment right now and pray again for God to make this dream a reality.

We now turn our attention to our third biblical parenting principal: *draw your child's heart to yours*. As we move forward in our journey, I will be increasingly encouraging you to take steps to connect with your son or daughter in new ways. Practicing the first two principles can be very hard. They force us to deal with deep and personal things that we often prefer to avoid. Practicing these last two principles will be a challenge as well, because now is the time to take courageous steps in loving, reaching out, speaking truth, and spending time with your adult children. For many parents the path ahead is filled with fear. We all fear rejection, anger, and grief, and none of us want to do anything that will make our relationships worse. As parents of wayward children, you don't want to push your children farther away. We must choose, though, to put aside our fears. The souls of our children hang in the balance. If we have a son or a daughter who is far from God, times are desperate! And desperate times call for desperate measures. It's not by accident that you're reading this book. God has given you a burden for the soul of your child, and He is preparing you, even now, for a new day of making an impact in the heart of your son or daughter for Christ.

THE SHORTEST DISTANCE

One of the most common prayers for a parent of an adult child who is far from God goes something like this: "Lord, please bring someone into my child's life who can help point _____ to Christ. Bring someone into my child's life who will be a good influence, rather than someone who will lead my child astray. Let _____ get connected with a Christian friend or a church group to help with spiritual growth. In Jesus' name, Amen."

There's nothing wrong with a prayer like this. If you've been praying this way, keep it up! But make no mistake—*you* are still a primary influence in your child's life. One of the enemy's lies is that you, as an empty-nest parent, have lost your chance to make a difference and point your son or daughter to Christ, and now all you can do is pray for him or her and hope that God brings someone else into your child's life to do what you could not do when your child was younger.

This is a lie. Here is the plain truth—the shortest distance between your child's heart and Christ is you.

Is it possible that God will bring someone else into your child's life who will lead him or her to the Lord? Of course—and we would all rejoice if that were to happen. God brings people to Christ through many different paths. But if someone else leads your child to deep faith in Christ, God would have chosen to lead your child the long way around. The shortest distance, the easiest path, the path with the greatest likelihood of success is you.

Here is the plain truth—the shortest distance between your child's heart and Christ is you.

God created the family, and He created parents to be the primary agent in passing faith to the next generation. God's plan is beautiful. He calls parents to love Him and follow Him. He calls children to give their hearts to their parents, and for parents then to pass the hearts of their children on to Christ. God has ordained parents with the mission and spiritual influence to impress the hearts of their children with a love for God—and this mission does not expire when children grow up and leave home. Your influence in the life of your child may look different now that your son or daughter is grown, but it hasn't diminished. In order to move forward, we need to reject the world's lie that our time has passed when it comes to influencing our children toward Christ. The best chance your child has in coming to Christ is *you*.

GIVE ME YOUR HEART

This third parenting principle—drawing your child's heart to yours—comes from the book of Proverbs. This is one of my favorite Scriptures on parenting: "The father of a righteous man has great joy; he who has a wise son delights in him. May your father and mother be glad; may she who gave you birth rejoice! My son, give me your heart" (23:24–26).

Most of the book of Proverbs was written by Solomon to his son. The last phrase above encapsulates the way Solomon pleads with this son throughout the book: "My son, give me your heart!" Solomon understood that God had called him to win the hearts of his children so that he could pass their hearts to God. Solomon made many tragic decisions in his life. He knew God, and knew the consequences of not obeying Him. Consider *how* Solomon wrote to his sons:

> Listen, my son, to your father's instruction and do not forsake your mother's teaching. (1:8)

> My son, do not forget my teaching, but keep my commands in your heart. (3:1)

> Listen, my sons, to a father's instruction; pay attention and gain understanding. (4:1)

> Now then, my sons, listen to me; blessed are those who keep my ways. (8:32)

He pleads with his sons, over and over again, to listen carefully to what he had to teach them. He was eager to have his children follow after God. Solomon knew that if he was to impress the hearts of his children with a love for God, he needed something. Look carefully at what Solomon wanted from his son in Proverbs 23:26, "My son, *give me your heart*" (emphasis added).

In Christian circles, one often hears the phrase *give your heart*, but when Christians say this, we refer to "giving your heart to Jesus." Not to trample on a sacred contemporary phrase, but *give your heart to Jesus* is not in the Bible. I'm not starting a crusade against Christians talking like this. When people use this concept of giving our hearts to Christ, they're talking about our need to repent, believe in Christ, and trust Him alone to save us. *Giving your heart* is, for better or worse, what people use to encapsulate those concepts. On the other hand, the Scriptures do speak about a relationship in which God does call us to give our hearts to someone. It is here in Proverbs 23. God wants children to give their hearts to their parents. God wants children to trust their parents with their deepest thoughts, fears, beliefs, and decisions.

A SPIRITUAL ATTACK POINT

If heart-connection is so vital in the parent–child relationship, we can expect Satan to do all he can to break it. The attacks start early. Our culture encourages kids even in elementary school to take their hearts away from their parents. The vast majority of the shows on TV present parents as "dorks" and "out of touch." Have you noticed how most evening TV programs rank the characters? At the top of the list is the family pet. The children are the highest-ranking human members of the family with the most wit, insight, wisdom, and solutions to the problems facing the family. Mom comes in after the kids, and dad brings up the rear with his pervasive incompetence, idiotic mistakes, and general buffoonery. Every day the world screams at our children, "Your parents are out of touch, out to lunch, and just don't get it! Your mission is to put up with them as best you can until you can escape."

Most parents begin to see the straining of the heart-connection with their children in the late elementary or early middle school years. Perhaps you've experienced a situation similar to this. You pick up your daughter from a church youth group event. She flops down next to you in the front seat of the car, and you pull away from the church. In a friendly tone you ask, "How was youth group tonight?" Pause. "Fine," she says as if she were half asleep. "What did you learn?" Pause. "Stuff." What's going on here? Why is she bristling? You're not being rude or invasive. You just want to talk with her about her night and to see how God might have worked in her life. Yet she sends the clear message, week after week, that she's not comfortable talking with you about these things. She does not want to give her heart to you.

The reason this conversation is so tense and difficult is because both parent and daughter are under intense spiritual attack. In the passenger seat, where the daughter sits, the attack goes something like this: "You don't talk with your father or mother about these things. It's okay to talk with your friends or with your youth leader. You can give your heart to them.

Don't give your heart to your father! Don't give your heart to your mother! It's none of their business. You're old enough now to make your own decisions. Faith is a personal thing. Keep it that way."

Over in the driver's seat, the enemy is pouring it on as well. The deception sounds something like this: "Don't you remember? Your child is now an adolescent. It's normal for kids not to like their parents and not to want to be with you. Friends are more important to kids at this age. You shouldn't pry. You'll only push your child away. You have to focus on just surviving these next ten years because your child wants nothing to do with you, your church, your God, and your values. The best you can hope for is that your child will have good Christian friends, so focus on getting your child into healthy environments. If you can survive, maybe someday you can have a good relationship again." As the lies settle into the hearts of parents, they slowly drift away from their children and stop asking the essential question, "Will you give me your heart?"

The myth of "adolescence" has taken such root in our culture that from the ages of twelve to twenty-two, we expect young men and women to act irresponsibly.

These lies are tied to what some have called *the myth of adolescence*.[1] During the twentieth century, sociologists developed a new category for people—adolescents. Prior to this, culture viewed each person as either a child or an adult. The myth of adolescence has taken such root in our culture today that from the ages of twelve to twenty-two, we *expect* young men and women to act irresponsibly, rebel against their parents, not enjoy being with their families, and reject the faith they were raised with.

Think of how far we've come! We hear the sad news that a twenty-two-year-old man got drunk and crashed his car. Are we shocked that a grown man would act so irresponsibly? No! The common response is, "Well, he's still a kid, and kids do stupid things. We can only hope that he'll learn his lesson." Our culture expects young people to rebel—and by and large, this generation of young people is living up to those expectations.

Some misguided youth leaders in the church fan the flame of this destructive deception. They believe that the teen years are the time when young people *won't* talk with their parents, so the leaders need to stand in as surrogates. Wise youth leaders, if they discover that teenagers don't have heart-connections with their parents, will make it their top priority to encourage students to give their hearts to their parents.[2] Godly leaders help teens focus on building relationships with their parents, and encourage students to open up to their moms and dads about everything in their lives.

Why does the enemy seek to break the heart-connection between parents and children right before the teen years? Because that's the time when our sons and daughters need us more than ever before. Teenagers are making decisions that can have an impact their entire lives. They need the love and guidance of their parents—the teen years are the worst time to push their parents away. Yet that's exactly what happens in millions of homes.

Imagine that you've chosen to scale Mount Everest. You've shelled out sixty thousand dollars to your Sherpa guides. After a few days, you finally arrive at twenty-six thousand feet above sea-level and are preparing to enter "the death zone." (If a climber is going to die on Everest, it's most likely to happen between twenty-six thousand feet and the summit.) Up until this point, you've been climbing well and feeling great. You've been doing so well, in fact, that your guides inform you that, because of your excellent physical conditioning and clear mountaineering skills, they're going back down to base camp and let you finish the climb on your own. How would you react? I'd be furious! I didn't pay sixty thousand dollars to get from sea level to twenty-six thousand feet. I paid to be guided through the death zone.

In some ways, the teen years are like that final stage of the climb. (This is not to say that parenting ends after our kids leave home. You wouldn't be reading this book if that were the case.)

As parenting becomes increasingly difficult, and as the heart-connection between parents and children comes under intense attack, many parents make the unfortunate choice of going back down to base camp and letting their teens climb to the summit on their own. These parents buy the lie that it's actually healthy for their teenagers to withdraw from them.[3]

Our children are best prepared for a blessed life and to have an impact in the world for Christ when their hearts are close to ours.

Our children are best prepared for a blessed life and to have an impact in the world for Christ when their hearts are close to ours. One of my favorite stories of the power of heart-connection is from the life of the famous Scottish missionary John G. Paton (1824–1907). The time had come for young John to leave home and set off for seminary in Glasgow. He was in his early twenties, which, in those days, was considered well into adulthood. From his hometown, it was a forty-mile walk to the train station. Forty years after he boarded that train, he wrote this account:

My dear father walked with me the first six miles of the way. His counsels and tears and heavenly conversation on that parting journey are fresh in my heart as if it had been but yesterday; and tears are on my cheeks as freely now as then, whenever memory steals me away to the scene. For the last half mile or so we walked on together in almost unbroken silence. . . . His lips kept moving in silent prayers for me; and his tears fell fast when our eyes met each other in looks for which all speech was vain! We halted on reaching the appointed parting place; he grasped my hand firmly for a minute in silence, and then solemnly and affectionately said: "God bless you, my son! Your father's God prosper you, and keep you from all evil!" Unable to say more, his lips kept moving in silent prayer; in tears we embraced, and parted. I ran off as fast as I could; and, when about to turn a corner in the road where he would lose sight of me, I looked back and saw him still standing with head uncovered where I had left him—gazing after me. Waving my hat in adieu, I rounded the corner and out of sight in an instant. But my heart was too full and sore to carry me further, so I darted into the side of the road and wept for a time. Then, rising up cautiously, I climbed the dike to see if he yet stood where I had left him; and just at that moment I caught a glimpse of him climbing the dyke and looking out for me! He did not see me, and after he gazed eagerly in my direction for a while, he got down, set his face toward home, and began to return—his head still uncovered, and his heart, I felt sure, still rising in prayers for me. I watched through blinding tears, till his form faded from my gaze; and then, hastening on my way, vowed deeply and oft, by the help of God, to live and act so as never to grieve or dishonor such a father and mother as he had given me.[4]

Perhaps you look back on your journey with your adult child and recognize that your heart-connection with your son or daughter began to separate during those late elementary or teen years. The breaking of the heart-connection with parents is Satan's first step to pulling the souls of children away from Christ. He seeks to replace warmth, honesty, trust, and closeness with lies, cover-ups, and privacy. Parents usually can sense this change happening. They become increasingly nervous and anxious about their children. They sense their sons or daughters keeping secrets from them, not sharing their struggles, keeping money private, and not always being where they said they would be.

WHY A HEART-CONNECTION MATTERS

If you want God to use you to encourage faith in your adult child, you must make it a priority to restore and deepen your heart-connection with your son or daughter. Why is this so essential? Influence flows through heart-connection.[5] You're reading this book because you want to *influence* your son or daughter and point his or her heart to Christ. We can't control the hearts of our children. All we have is influence, and influence flows through a warm heart-connection.

Imagine that you had two neighbors. The neighbor on your right is one of the rudest people you know. He routinely mocks you, laughs at you, and curses at you. He's stolen your property, spread lies about you to the neighborhood, and glares at you when you're both outside. The neighbor on your left is one of your closest friends. He's always there when you need a hand. He asks how he can be praying for you and your family. He's shown himself trustworthy as you've faced difficult situations. He's forgiven you for some mistakes that you've made in the past. The two neighbors could not be more different.

One day, on the way home from the store, you get into a fender bender. You can still drive the car, but it looks pretty banged up. You limp the car home and pull into your driveway. Your rude neighbor immediately walks over to you and says, "Looks like you had an accident. I recommend that you go see Mike down at Central Body Shop. He does good work." How would you respond? My guess is that you'd grit your teeth, get the conversation over as quickly as possible without being overly rude, and get inside. You'd probably also immediately reject any advice he gave to you.

Now rewind the tape. You come home with the banged up car, but this time your nice neighbor comes out to meet you. He says, "Looks like you had an accident. I recommend that you go see Mike down at Central Body Shop. He does good work." Notice he said the exact same thing the other guy did, but wouldn't you respond differently? Yes! "Thanks for coming over. This was the last thing I needed today, and I really didn't know who to call. I'll call this Mike guy right away. I appreciate your advice." The truth is, your rude neighbor may have given you excellent advice. His attempt to *influence* you to take your car to a good shop may have been totally valid, but there was no way you'd ever allow yourself to *be influenced* by such a person. This is because influence flows through heart-connection. Influence flows best through a warm, close, caring relationship.

That is what our third principle, *draw your child's heart to yours*, is all about. You must be intentional about doing all you can to restore and rebuild a warm relationship with your adult son or daughter. This is a prerequisite if you want to influence your wayward child's heart toward Christ. You must begin with the mission, "My son, give me your heart!"

REPAIRING BROKEN FOUNDATIONS

Think of this heart-connection between you and your child like a bridge. It's a bridge that connects you in relationship with one another. Warmth, honesty, influence, love, and support flow across the bridge. For many of you, this heart-connection bridge has collapsed, either completely or in vital sections.

When a bridge collapses, teams of engineers arrive on the scene to survey the damage, diagnose the problem, and oversee the process of reconstruction. Many bridges are strong above ground, but collapse because of faulty foundations. When a bridge is rebuilt, the foundation is repaired first. If the repair crews deal with all the problems above the ground, but fail to deal with the foundation issues, all their work will be wasted. In the same way, the first step to rebuilding the relationship-bridge between you and your child is to repair and strengthen the foundation.

Asking Our Children to Forgive Us

In the previous chapter we learned about the importance of forgiving our children for the things they've done to hurt us. We've considered God's plan of forgiveness, which is His gift to us to set us free from bitterness and resentment. We also faced the reality that true reconciliation with those who have hurt us is outside of our control. If our children have sinned against us and never repent and ask for our forgiveness, the relationships cannot be completely restored.

While it's true that full reconciliation depends on the repentance of our children... it also depends on us. We've all done things—or failed to do things—that have hurt our children. God calls *them* to forgive us for the ways that we've hurt them. Many of you probably went through a process of forgiving your parents for things that hurt you when you were growing up. As the burden lies with your children to take responsibility for the things they've done to hurt you and to ask your forgiveness, the burden lies with you to take responsibility for the things you've done to hurt your children and to ask for their forgiveness.

Do you remember the three questions we considered in chapter 4?

- How many of you were perfect parents? (None of us!)
- How many of you did some things wrong as a parent? (All of us!)
- Can you name the things you did wrong?

This third question is uncomfortable, isn't it? None of us likes to get specific about the things that we've done wrong. We're much more comfortable speaking in generalities. I hope you took the time in our earlier chapter to offer your heart to the Lord in repentance for the things that you named. Praise God that His mercies are new every morning, and His forgiveness never runs dry.

We need, though, to add a fourth question to the list. This question will make things even more uncomfortable, but it propels us toward rebuilding the foundations of the relationships with our children.

- Have you shared with your children the things you named in answer to the third question?

We're not totally responsible for the choices that our children have made, but we are partially responsible. The things we've done to hurt them ... have hurt them. We've hurt them, and hurt our relationships with them. Thank God for the gift of forgiveness and reconciliation! Do you want to rebuild the broken foundation of your relationship with your son or daughter? Do for your child what perhaps you're waiting for your child to do for you. Share with your son or daughter the things that you wish you'd done differently. Apologize to your child for the things that you believe you did wrong as a parent. Ask your son or daughter to forgive you. Remember, underneath a person's intellectual rejection of Christ is personal pain. Anytime we help our children forgive and heal from their life-wounds, we soften their hearts toward God.

In my family, I'm trying to practice asking forgiveness on an ongoing basis. It's brutally difficult for two reasons. One, I do a lot of things wrong. (I guess that gives me a lot of practice at repenting.) Two, I'm prideful, defensive, and don't like to admit I'm wrong. Not a great combination. I'm praying that God will give me the grace to apologize as I go and not leave my children with a backlog of hurt feelings that we haven't reconciled. I regularly have to ask forgiveness for using a harsh tone of voice with my kids. I find that I'm at my worst when I'm trying to do too many things at the same time, and I end up snapping at them or at Amy. I so much want God to help me be the kind of man who can quickly see when I've sinned, and to say, "I was harsh with you. That was wrong of me. I shouldn't talk to you like that. Will you please forgive me?"

Amy and I also use the question from Proverbs 23:26 when we apologize to our kids. "Will you give your heart back to me?" After I've yelled at one of my kids, they're visibly upset and withdrawn from me. This question, "Will you give your heart back to me?" is packed with the power of reconciliation.

Apologizing the Right Way

There are at least three categories of families when it comes to apologies. The first kind of family is easy to recognize; they don't apologize at all. People in these families can hardly ever remember their own parents or siblings saying, "I'm sorry," or "I was wrong." Perhaps you grew up in a home like this.

The second category of family has followed in the mold of the elementary school playground when it comes to apologizing. Think back with me. Two boys get into a fracas near the jungle gym. They start pushing and shoving each other, and pretty soon they're wrestling in the wood chips. The other kids start chanting "fight!" and soon a teacher is on the scene. He breaks up the boys, gets things calmed down, and at the end of his lecture he says, "Now you boys say you're sorry." The boys glare at each other and with teeth clenched say, "Sorry." With that the teacher says, "Good boys, now run along!" Yes, the boys uttered the word *sorry*, but what they really meant with their eyes and with their tone was, "I hate you!"

The world has taught us a terribly shallow and inadequate way of resolving conflict. The person who did something wrong says, "I'm sorry." The person who was wronged says, "It's okay." That's it. So many families depend on that insignificant exchange to resolve and reconcile their relationships after someone has been hurt. Our culture has robbed us of a biblical way of apologizing and asking forgiveness.

I want my family—and yours—to be in the third category... a family that frequently and comfortably uses biblical language in seeking and receiving forgiveness. The next step in our journey is to put this into practice. If we want to rebuild the foundations of the relationship bridges between us and our children, the first step may be asking for their forgiveness for the things that we've done to hurt them. You can do this in person or over the phone if necessary. Don't use a letter for this. Forgiveness is deeply personal and should be asked for, given, and received personally. It's important to plan what you're going to say and to discipline yourself to use biblical language. If you're not careful, your attempt at an apology can cause more hurt than it heals.

I encourage you to consider writing down the words that you want to say to your child. This written draft will help you when you talk face-to-face. The four steps that follow are packed with reconciliation power!

The first step to a biblical apology is to confess—or simply to state what you did or didn't do. The word *confession* means to "say with" or "agree with." When we confess sin to God, we agree with Him that what we did was wrong. Simple statements of confession might sound like this:

"Son, I didn't lead our family spiritually."

"Daughter, I was more interested in succeeding in my job than with my family."

"Son, I didn't prioritize respecting your father the way I should have."

"Daughter, I'm sorry that I was more concerned about ministering to our neighbors than ministering to you."

"Son, I was angry and harsh with you."

"Daughter, I physically hurt you."

"Son, I didn't tell you that I loved you."

"Daughter, I made you feel like nothing was ever good enough for me. I was a perfectionist, and that crushed your spirit."

If you're having a hard time with what to say, go back to the questions we considered earlier. Were you a perfect parent? Did you do things wrong as a parent? Can you name these things? Whatever you would *name* is what needs to be confessed. Be as specific as you can.

After you've stated simply the things you did or didn't do, it's of the utmost importance that you don't make any excuses. Do *not* say things like this:

"But I was going through a hard time back then."

"But I was doing the best I knew how."

"But you have to understand I didn't have a good example of how to be a parent."

"But I wasn't a Christian when you were growing up."

All these circumstances may be true and legitimate factors that contributed to your choices, but they're not relevant in this conversation. Not only are they not relevant, but they will immediately cause your child's heart to focus on your excuse rather than your confession. As a result, your attempt to rebuild the foundation of your relationship will have the opposite effect.

Rather than drawing your child's heart to yours, you'll push it away.

Next say, "I was wrong." This is an easy one. Right after you go through your confession, simply say, "I was wrong." Well... maybe it's not so easy. I'm amazed at how many seemingly mature Christian adults are incapable of uttering these three little words: "I was wrong." Try it right now. If people are around you, you can just whisper it so they don't think you're crazy. See how the words feel coming out of your mouth... "I was wrong." Now think carefully. When was the last time you said this to someone? Everyone acknowledges that they make mistakes (translation—they do some things that are wrong). Yet hardly anyone ever utters the words, "What I did was wrong!" These are powerful words, particularly when they come from a heart of godly sorrow.

The next step is to say, "I am sorry." For most people, this is all they say when they apologize. When *I am sorry* is used alone, it carries very little weight. When it is said within the context of a biblical apology, it is valuable.

The last step is to ask, "Will you please forgive me?" This is the million-dollar question when we seek to rebuild the broken foundations of a relationship. After we confess what we have done and not done, after we humbly acknowledge that those things were wrong, and that we are truly sorry, we then have the opportunity to ask the people we have hurt if they would be willing to give us a gift. Will you forgive me?

It's one of the most powerful questions that can be asked. The answer either brings precious joy or deep pain. The question is so powerful that I encourage you to give plenty of time to your son or daughter before they answer it. You may say something like this: "Thank you for listening to my confession, _____. It means a lot to me that I can share these things with you. I'm about to ask you a very important question. It's so important that I don't want you to answer it right away. You may need a few days to think about it, so please don't answer if you don't want to. The last thing I want to do is pressure you. Here's the question: Will you please forgive me?"

Richard's Heartfelt Apology

Richard came to Christ later in life. In his first marriage, prior to his conversion, he made choices that hurt his son Steven. While Richard and his son have a cordial relationship today, Steven is far from God. Richard knew if he was to point his son's heart to Christ, he needed to deal with the past. He chose to write down his thoughts so that he could clearly communicate them to his son at his next visit. Here is what Richard shared:

> I remember once in the car, harshly yelling my lungs out at you to be quiet and reaching around and grabbing you by the arm, shaking you to be quiet, all the while driving along crazily, putting the whole family at risk. I had promised myself that I would never treat my kids the way I was treated. That day, I broke that promise.
>
> I was critical of you for the way you played catch with me. Of course, your vision problem (later corrected by surgery) just might have had something to do with it. It just might be that one needs to see correctly in order to catch a ball. I am so ashamed of myself for that condescending attitude. I am sure it hurt you.
>
> I did not stay in the hospital overnight with you to comfort you when you eventually had corrective eye surgery. Someone gave you a stuffed teddy bear to fill my rightful place.
>
> I was not at home, but was taking a walk with your mom, when some neighborhood boys attacked you. Your knee was cut open when they pushed you, and you fell on the metal edging around the lawn. You suffered alone at the emergency room until a neighbor located us and we arrived to give permission for the doctors to treat you. I passed out when the doctor began to examine your wound, and I saw your torn flesh and blood, and felt your pain when he cranked the joint.

I remember the coin-purse wound opening and closing during his manipulation, and I just lost it. Even worse, I did not have the guts to call the police or confront the boys' parents about their bully sons.

Later, I was unfaithful to your mother, broke our wedding vows, and eventually destroyed our beautiful little family. I was spiritually ignorant, self-focused, and dead wrong.

Although I fulfilled all my child-support requirements, I backed away from being involved in you and your sister's lives. I was a coward in dealing with your mother's anger and hurt, and in dealing with the huge pain and disappointment my choices had created in your lives.

I still think of the beautiful painting you did from a picture of yourself as a little guy of three or four years old. I remember the guilt I felt for being responsible for the angry expression on your face. Things were wrong in our family between your mother and me, mostly because of me, but I could finally "see" the effect it was having on my children by that pained look. I had been completely callous to your needs and the needs of your sister and your mother.

I am most sorry that I did not know Jesus Christ at that time of life. I was so arrogant, selfish, and self-centered about my career. I had a "me, me, me" focus on getting ahead, and on doing things my way. I had turned my back on all the religious background I was exposed to as a child. So very little of what I did as a husband to your mom and as a dad to you was pleasing to God. I wish I had a second chance to do things over again.

Steven, I am very sorry for all these things I have shared with you and the pain and loss they caused you. They were wrong, and I was wrong. I want to ask you something very important, but I don't want you to answer me now unless you feel you want to. Feel free to take days or weeks to give me your answer; because this is a very important question... will you please forgive me?

Who Goes First?

Think for a moment how much it would mean to you if your son or your daughter came to you with a spirit of humility and repentance and asked your forgiveness for the things he or she had done to hurt you. What a blessing that would be... almost too good to be true. It may feel like you've been waiting forever for it to happen. My guess is that your child feels the exact same way... waiting, hoping beyond hope, that you will come to him or her, acknowledge the things that you have done to hurt your child, and ask for his or her forgiveness.

> *You're waiting for your child to repent. Your son or daughter is waiting for you to repent. Who will make the first move?*

So who should go first? You're waiting for your child to repent. Your son or daughter is waiting for you to repent. Who will make the first move? Let us as fathers and mothers follow in the example of our heavenly Father—humble ourselves, take the initiative, and pursue reconciliation with our children. God can use your repentance to help draw your child's heart to yours and ultimately point your child's heart to Christ.

Questions for Reflection/Discussion

1. In what ways does our culture communicate to empty-nest parents that your time of influence has passed?
2. How were apologies handled in the home you grew up in? What steps can you take to help your family and extended family improve how the family deals with hurt and conflict?
3. What is the hardest part about trying to have spiritual conversations with your son or daughter?

Chapter 8

REBUILDING THE BRIDGE

CHRISTOPHER IS IN HIS late seventies. He came to Christ fifteen years ago. His children are all in their forties. Here is his story in his own words:

> When I came to Christ, my kids were nowhere spiritually. They had endured a terrible divorce between me and their mother, who was an alcoholic. After I came to the Lord, I bought them Bibles, invited them to church, and gave them religious books for their birthdays. I knew that I had to pray, but also that I had to put action to my prayers. My children knew me for over forty years apart from Christ. I knew their journey to Christ would not happen overnight.
>
> I have been blessed with a close relationship with my three boys. I am grateful that they treat me with respect and that we can talk together. I know I need to use that influence and have the courage to speak up and talk with them about spiritual things. I asked my oldest son to attend church with me. I wanted to share that experience with him, and for him to meet my friends. He came, sat with his arms folded, and was courteous to my friends. Then my son found out that he had a heart problem. There are no atheists in fox holes! He called me and told me he was ready to go to church with me on Easter. It was a positive sign to me that he reacted to a crisis by taking a step toward God.

One of the most difficult conversations I have had with my children is to apologize to them for not doing everything I could to save my first marriage. I was wrong about how much the divorce would affect them.

Thankfully, one of my sons married a Christian woman. The Lord is moving in on my whole family, one person at a time. I am seventy-seven years old now. Time is short. I want to be in heaven with my children and grandchildren. I am going to try and convince them that they need to give their best to important things and to eternity. Right now their focus is on business, material things, and entertainment. I pray for God to make me a loving father. I do know that my children have had conversations between them about how "dad is different now." God gets credit for that. I don't want God's work in my life to be just for me; I want it to spill over into my children, their spouses, my grandchildren, and beyond.

In the previous chapter we looked at a third biblical parenting principle—drawing our children's hearts to ours. We learned how influence flows through heart-connection. When we have a warm, close, open, loving relationship, we have influence. Heart-connection is like a bridge between two people, over which crosses encouragement, mentorship, influence, and spiritual discipleship. Many parents with adult children face the challenge of seeking to influence their children without a strong relationship-bridge. I hope that you took some bold steps in an effort to repair any crumbled foundations under the bridge between you and your son or daughter. After we've shored up the foundations, we can begin rebuilding the relationship bridge as we embrace this biblical call to draw our children's hearts to ours.

REBUILDING ACTION PLAN #1
Communicate honestly with your son or daughter about the fears and anxieties you have in regards to talking with him or her about spiritual things.

I encourage you to have a conversation with your son or daughter that goes something like this:

> I would like to talk with you about something that I'm very nervous about. I'm uncomfortable even bringing this up with you. I feel like sometimes when I try to talk with you about personal things, it doesn't go very well. If I try to talk about spiritual things, it goes even worse. I sometimes feel that I'm annoying you, or even angering you, and then I don't respond well. I sometimes get sad or angry myself. Then we both go away from the conversation in a bad place. You're angry and I'm sad. This seems to keep happening over and over again, and I don't really know all the reasons why. What I do know is that I want to have the kind of relationship with you in which we can talk openly and honestly about personal things. I'd love to have a better relationship with you, and for both of us to feel more comfortable being open with each other. I don't know how to do that, but it's what I want. I can tell that some of these conversations aren't very pleasant for you, so I would imagine that you'd like to find a new way for us to relate to each other, too. What do you think?

The goal of starting a conversation with these words is not to fix the situation—or to fix your child. The goal is trying to draw your child's heart to yours. This is a way to communicate to your son or daughter that you understand that the current state of the relationship isn't working well, and you'd like things to be different.

REBUILDING ACTION PLAN #2

Invite your son or daughter to be honest with you about his or her fears and anxieties in regards to talking with you about spiritual things.

Here's a way that you can follow up on the action plan above. You may move right into this as a part of a larger discussion, or save it for another time. Consider initiating the following conversation with your child:

Can I ask you a question? I want to give you fair warning, the question is a little unusual, but it would mean a lot to me if you'd tell me what you think. Here it is—how comfortable do you feel talking with me about personal things or even spiritual things? Let me ask it this way. On a scale of one to ten, with ten being totally comfortable and one being not comfortable at all, how comfortable do you feel talking about personal and religious things with me?

Be prepared for an awkward pause. Imagine that your son or daughter responded by saying, "Well, Mom, to be honest, I would have to say... three." Imagine that no sooner is the number *three* out of our child's mouth that you launch into a tearful speech: "Three! How could you possibly say three? Haven't I always told you from the time you were little that you can always tell me anything! You know that you can always tell me the truth! And now you say *three*. How did this happen?"

It's highly likely that a child would respond with a three because of a history of hearing speeches like that. The attempt at having a meaningful conversation to draw the child's heart to his or her parent, from the child's perspective, has turned into another guilt trip.

Let's look at this situation from a different perspective. You take the risk and ask your child on a scale of one to ten how comfortable he or she feels talking with you about spiritual things. Your son or daughter indicates a three. At this point, don't miss the beautiful thing that just happened. Your child gave you a piece of his or her heart and was honest with you. That's *exactly* what you were looking for. You should respond positively:

Thank you for telling me the truth. I think a lot of young people would just tell me what I want to hear. You didn't do that. They would say eight, nine, or ten. You had the guts to tell me the truth. You made the choice to tell me something I didn't want to hear. That means a lot to me. Now, I want to understand where you're coming from. Can you tell me more about why you said *three*?

Then be very quiet and listen for as long as it takes. Keep yourself focused on the purpose of the conversation. You're seeking to draw your child's heart to yours. If your son or daughter is talking and being honest with you about personal things, God is on the move.

Here is another set of questions that may help you draw your child's heart to yours:

> I have a personal question to ask you. I don't mean to make you feel uncomfortable, but it would mean a lot to me to have your honest answer. _____, do you know that I love you?

> If your child is willing to let you even ask this question, he or she will likely respond with a cautious "yes." I'm glad to hear you say that, because I do love you. Now I have one more question for you, and this one may be harder to answer, but again I really want to hear the truth. Do you *feel* loved by me? I know you said that you know I love you... but do you *feel* loved by me?

You'd be surprised how many grown children will say that they have no doubts that their parents love them, but that they don't feel loved. They believe the love is there intellectually, but experientially, it's another story.

If your son or daughter was honest enough to say, "Well... no... I guess I don't always feel loved by you," be prepared to ask the key question to draw his or her heart to yours: "Thank you for being willing to tell me the truth. I'm sorry to hear that you don't always feel loved by me. Can you tell me more? Help me understand your feelings..."

It's vital that you adapt this new way of responding when your son or daughter says things you don't want to hear. I'm not talking about ignoring rudeness or disrespect, but when your child expresses an honest viewpoint, opinion, or perspective, even if it's something that you totally disagree with, it indicates that the relationship bridge may be in repair. Do everything you can to elevate the value of honesty in the relationship.

Seek honesty at all costs. Pray for honesty at all costs.

Let's say that your son has rejected Christianity and is following an Eastern religion. You and he are better off if he's honest, communicative, and clear with you about his spiritual choice than if he lied to you and told you that he loved Jesus, while he secretly pursued his false religion. Seek honesty at all costs. Pray for honesty at all costs.

Let's say that this son begins an effort to persuade you to believe in the Eastern religion, too. Before you get into a theological debate, consider responding this way:

> Son, I first want to say that I'm grateful we can talk about deep and important things like this. It means the world to me that you would open up your heart to me and share with me your deepest beliefs. We may not agree on things right now, but even if we disagree about every single thing for the rest of our lives, I want to have a close relationship with you in which we can always share our hearts and be honest with each other. Now, tell me more about what has drawn you to these new beliefs...

Honesty may hurt you deeply, but when our children are honest with us about their true thoughts, feelings, convictions, and choices, we have a growing heart-connection with them... and through heart-connection flows influence.

REBUILDING ACTION PLAN #3

Focus on speaking with extra respect to sons and extra gentleness to daughters.

One of Satan's lies that has taken root in our secular culture is that boys and girls, men and women are the same. The Bible teaches that men and women were created with equal value, worth, dignity, and importance. Now, after the fall, we are equally sinful. But we were also created differently. We are different biologically and psychologically because God created men and women for equally important but very different roles. Parents should not treat boys and girls the same. The masculine soul and the feminine soul are built by God to reflect complimentary strength and beauty. In the excellent book *Love and Respect*, Emerson Eggerich teaches about marriage from Ephesians 5:33, where husbands are commanded to love their wives, and wives are commanded to respect their husbands. Eggerich rightly suggests that in the same way husbands thrive and respond to respect from their wives, sons thrive and respond to respect from their parents. Similarly, wives thrive and respond to love and gentleness from their husbands, and therefore daughters thrive and respond to love and gentleness from their parents.[1]

If you have a son, what grade would you give yourself in regard to showing respect to him and speaking to him with a respectful tone? If you think little boys respond poorly when they are disrespected, try showing disrespect to a grown man! What happens when a grown son feels like his mother or his father is treating him like a little kid? He immediately gets tense, resistant, and may even become angry. Men are particularly sensitive to disrespect because of how God created the masculine soul. I'm not saying that boys don't want to be treated with love and gentleness; rather, when a man is treated with respect, he generally responds in kind. If you're up for a real challenge, ask your son this:

> Son, I've been thinking. I realize that it's very important for me to treat you with respect. You're a grown man, and I never want to talk down to you or treat you like a child. Do you feel that I treat you and speak to you with respect?

I want to speak specifically to fathers for a moment. Never underestimate the power and influence of your words. When you walk into a store and look at all the items on the shelves, you notice that some are expensive and some are cheap. Why? What determines how valuable things are? Two fundamental economic principles drive value: supply and demand. How much will you pay me for a bucket of dirt? You'll probably pay nothing. Why? Because there's a huge supply of dirt and very low demand, which makes a bucket of dirt next to worthless. On the other hand, how much will you pay me for a bucket of diamonds? You probably couldn't afford it. Why? Because the supply of diamonds is very low and the demand is very high, which makes them extremely valuable and extremely expensive.

When something is in high demand and low supply, it is precious and valuable.

Consider with me the value of a father's words. In a typical home, is there a high supply or a low supply of a father's words of spiritual nurture, guidance, and encouragement for his wife and children? Typically, the supply is low. On the other hand, what is the desire for these words from his wife and children? The demand is extremely high. What does this mean? Low supply, high demand... a father's words of spiritual nurture and instruction are powerful and priceless.

When something is in high demand and low supply, it is precious and valuable. Boys have a God-given, high desire to receive respect from their family members. Many sons, though, rarely receive words of respect at home from parents and siblings. High demand. Low supply. Any gesture you make to treat your son with respect can have a powerful influence in his life and in your relationship. Sons who are treated with respect are much more likely to respond to their parents with warmth, love, and respect. Does your son work hard at his job? Say, "I want you to know that I respect how hard you work, and that you take your job seriously." Does he treat you cordially even though he is struggling spiritually? Tell him, "I know that we have our differences, but I admire the fact that you treat me with respect. That means a lot to me." Does your son try to be involved in the lives of his children? Affirm him by saying, "I have a lot of respect for how committed you are to spending time with your children. A lot of men these days don't take their responsibilities as a dad as seriously as you do. I am proud of you for that."

If you have a daughter, what grade would you give yourself in regard to showing her gentleness and love? Think back to how your daughter responded to other girls in the neighborhood if she thought they were mean to her. She was devastated. God built the feminine soul to respond to love and gentleness. Think of your history with your daughter. Have you ever seen a situation in which your daughter responded positively to harshness from you? Again, I'm not saying that women do not want to be respected. Everyone wants to be treated with respect. The point here is that God created women in such a way that they respond with warmth, love, and closeness when someone treats them with gentleness and love. Are you ready for the challenge? Ask your daughter something like this:

> Daughter, I've been thinking. I realize that it's very important for me to treat you with gentleness and love. I never want to be harsh or mean with you. I never want you to feel unsafe with me. Do you feel that I treat you and speak to you with gentleness and love?

The supply and demand principle applies here as well. Our daughters greatly desire to be treated with gentleness and love. That desire is built into their hearts by God. On the other hand, women are surrounded in our secular culture with crassness, rudeness, and talk that is anything but gentle. Many daughters grow up in homes where gentleness and love are rare. High demand. Low supply. We must learn from this! We must go out of our way to intentionally, regularly, and strategically communicate gentleness and love to our daughters. God calls us to draw the hearts of our daughters closer to us. Harshness is the quickest way to drive a daughter's heart into retreat. Daughters who are treated with gentleness are much more likely to respond to their parents with warmth, love, and respect.

REBUILDING ACTION PLAN #4

Seek to understand before seeking to be understood.

In the next chapter we move to our fourth biblical principle, *point your child's heart to Christ.* Many parents are eager for opportunities to speak to their children about Christ and to encourage them to trust Him. But when it comes to encouraging faith in adult children, we must make sure we're focused on understanding our children, not just being understood *by* them.

I've spent many hours interviewing twenty-somethings who grew up in the church but have walked away from faith in Christ. A running theme with these men and women is, "My parents just don't understand me. They're constantly trying to lecture me, fix me, and change me." Let's imagine that these adult children have ten interactions with their parents over the course of a few months. Many sons and daughters share the opinion that nine of these interactions and conversations are parents sitting their children down to express Mom's or Dad's concerns. The longer this pattern continues, the greater the child's resistance becomes to having a close relationship. When you call your child and say, "I was wondering if we might be able to get together this weekend and spend some time together," they hear you saying, "I want to sit you down to lecture you!"

> To draw your child's heart to yours, you must commit yourself to giving maximum effort to understanding your son or daughter, not just seeking to be understood by him or her.

How do we feel when friends, co-workers, or spouses are continually trying to ram something down our throats? We become increasingly resistant to the relationship and try to avoid them. If you want to draw your child's heart to yours and rebuild the relationship bridge of heart-connection, you must commit yourself to giving maximum effort to understanding your son or daughter, not just seeking to be understood by him or her. We'll need to commit to listening to our children before our children can open their hearts to receive our words and influence.

Here's a way you can begin to reverse this unhealthy pattern in many parent–child relationships. Consider saying something like this to your son or daughter:

> I've been thinking, _____. As I look at the way we relate to each other, it seems to me that I do a whole lot of talking and you do a whole lot of listening. If I were in your shoes, I think I might feel that I was being talked down to or lectured. I don't know if you ever feel like this with me. It's important to me, especially now that you're an adult, that you feel listened to and understood by me. I'd like to hear what you think about all this. Would you say that "I get it" and that I understand you, or am I on to something here that perhaps I'm doing too much talking and not enough listening?

If your son or daughter says, "You're a great listener, and I feel that you really understand me and where I am in my life," praise the Lord! If that is his or her response, then you know that this part of your relationship bridge is strong. But your child could say, "I'm not sure. I feel that there are parts of my life you understand, but other parts, not so much." This is still an excellent response. Why? Because your child let you into his or her heart. You got the truth. That is your cue to draw your child's heart to yours. Here's a prime opportunity to respond like this:

> Thanks for telling me the truth. I appreciate that so much. I'm really going to work on listening to you more. I hope a few months down the road, when I ask you this question again, you feel like I really understand you. I'm not expecting that we'll agree about everything, but at the very least, I want you to feel that I've taken the time to listen to you and to understand where you're coming from.

After you have the above conversation and you discover there is an understanding gap, here is a practical suggestion for listening and building understanding in your relationship with your adult child. Go to your son or daughter and express this:

> I want to ask a favor of you. If you don't want to do this, no problem. It would mean a lot to me if we could sit down at the kitchen table for ten minutes and for you to talk to me about anything you want to talk about. Whatever you want to say, you can say it. I really want to understand more of what's going on in your life, and all I want to do is listen. I promise I'm not going to interrupt you, question you, or lecture you after you're done. When the ten minutes are up, if you're done talking, I'll just say, "Thanks for telling me all that. I appreciate it," and we'll be done. What do you think?

If you're going to try this, start practicing biting your tongue. Literally. Bite it gently. Hold it between your teeth. Why practice biting your tongue? It's likely during these ten minutes that your son or daughter will say something to which you feel you simply *must* respond. Remind yourself of the purpose of this conversation. The purpose is not to get into a conversation! This is about one thing... asking your child to give you his or her heart. This is about building the relationship bridge and strengthening your heart-connection so that your son or daughter is increasingly open to your godly influence.

As we prepare to move to our final principle, *pointing your child's heart to Christ*, take a few moments and pray for the goal of our journey:

> Lord, it's the desire of my heart and greatest prayer that my child, _____, would love You wholeheartedly. I pray that _____ would fully trust in Jesus Christ, and that by Your grace we would arrive safely home in heaven together. I can't do these things. Only You can. I ask in faith for You to work this miracle of grace and salvation in the life of my child. I pray this in the name of Jesus. Amen.

Questions for Reflection/Discussion

1. How would you describe the current health of the heart-connection between you and your child?
2. What has happened to make that heart-connection weak or strong?
3. As you read this chapter, which of the approaches to rebuilding heart-connection motivated you the most?
4. What are some ways that you have approached your son or daughter in the past that you believe did more harm than good?

Chapter 9

POINT YOUR CHILD'S HEART TO CHRIST

THUS FAR IN OUR journey we've explored three biblical parenting principles. We began with offering our hearts to the Lord through prayer and repentance. We then sought to turn our hearts to our children, asking God for a spirit of compassion, and forgiving them for the things they've done to hurt us. Our third principle is to draw our children's hearts to ours by repairing the broken foundations of our relationships, and committing ourselves to deepening the heart-connections between us. We now come to the fourth and final[1] principle—*point your child's heart to Christ.*

You may have expected the book to begin with this principle. The route of our journey, however, is vitally important. If we try to point our child's heart to Christ without offering our hearts to the Lord, we'll be accused of hypocrisy. If we do not first turn our hearts to our children in a spirit of commitment and compassion, we'll be accused of "shoving religion down their throats." If we do not seek to draw our children's heart to ours, the words we share with them will come from afar.

If you've skimmed through the previous principles, or haven't dedicated time to putting them into practice, I encourage you to stop reading. Go back and walk through the first three principles again and act on them. You'll never feel that you're "done" with any of them. These principles are not a scientific formula or step-by-step recipe in which you check things off as you go. The question is, have you taken steps and made progress in offering your heart to the Lord, turning your heart to your child, and drawing your child's heart to yours? If so, let's move into the fourth principle: *point your child's heart to Christ*. It's time to talk about making the brave choice to talk directly with your son or daughter about spiritual things and to encourage your son or daughter to put his or her faith and trust in Christ alone.

BE NOT ASHAMED OF THE GOSPEL

If you choose to take the tremendous risk of directly talking with your child about his or her relationship with God, Satan will shift his attack into high gear. He'll throw everything at you, beginning with fear and shame. You'll need to follow Christ's example and fight temptation using God's Word. I encourage you to post this verse on your bathroom mirror and computer desktop. Speak it out loud daily. God's Word alone can equip you for the journey ahead. Commit this verse to memory: "I am not ashamed of the gospel, because it is the power of God for the salvation of everyone who believes" (Rom. 1:16).

When we talk with our children about God, God's Word, and God's salvation through Jesus Christ alone, we have nothing to be ashamed of. We've been talking about our desire to *influence* the hearts of our children to love the Lord. What power do we have to change their hearts? The power does not lie with us, but rather in the Word of God. When the gospel is clearly spoken and when the Scriptures are shared, the Holy Spirit of God is at work.

> For the word of God is living and active. Sharper than any double-edged sword, it penetrates even to dividing soul and

spirit, joints and marrow; it judges the thoughts and attitudes of the heart. Nothing in all creation is hidden from God's sight. Everything is uncovered and laid bare before the eyes of him to whom we must give account. (Heb. 4:12–13)

God will give us opportunities to share the gospel with our children. We don't need to be creative or give dramatic illustrations and analogies. We can't make the good news more powerful or persuasive than it already is: God created the world. Man sinned. The fair penalty for all sin is death and eternal separation from God. By God's grace He made a way for us to be saved. God chose to become a man in Jesus Christ, take our sins upon Himself on the cross, and to pay the death penalty on our behalf. Jesus satisfied the justice of God, and rose again from the dead. We are forgiven, saved from hell, and saved for heaven when we respond to God's grace and put our full faith and trust in Christ, and Christ alone. We can choose to pay for our own sins, or repent and accept in faith Jesus' payment on our behalf.

If the Lord blesses you with the opportunity to explain the gospel to your adult child—a message he or she may have heard hundreds of times—have the courage to ask for a response: "_____, I believe that everything I've just told you about salvation is true. I want to be in heaven with you, and I want to ask you right now, are you ready to respond to God's grace, repent, and trust Christ as your Lord and Savior?"

Do you remember the earlier testimony of Abraham Piper? He pleads to parents of prodigal children:

> Point them to Christ. Your rebellious child's real problem is not drugs or sex or cigarettes or porn or laziness or crime or cussing or slovenliness or homosexuality or being in a punk band.... The best thing you can do for wayward children—and the only reason to follow any of these suggestions—is to show them Christ. It won't be simple or immediate, but the sins in their lives that distress you and destroy them will begin to disappear only when they see Jesus more as He actually is.[2]

I'm hesitant to use this next illustration because for many people it's all too real. But imagine for a moment that your child has a terminal illness. Time is short. Miraculously, you discover there is a cure for the illness! You rush to your son or daughter and say, "I've found the cure for your illness! I love you so much! You're going to live!" With disdain your child responds, "Cure? I'm not even sick. Frankly, I'm offended that you even think I'm sick. All you do is criticize me." Stunned, you reply, "You don't want the cure? You *are* sick. It's very serious. I love you and want you to get well." Your child spits back, "Leave me alone! Don't ever talk to me again about this so-called cure for an illness I don't even have."

What would you say then? Would you agree with your child? "Okay, I don't want to make you feel uncomfortable or drive you away from me. I won't bring it up again." Not a chance! You'd try again. Then you'd try again, and again, and again. When it comes to matters of life and death, nothing would stop you from doing everything in your power to help your child. If we would be this dedicated to the temporary life of our children's body, how much more passionate and committed should we be to the salvation of their immortal souls?

Yet, for all the love you have for your children, God loves them even more. God is pursuing the heart of your child infinitely more than you are. This is good news. Encouraging faith in your adult child is not *your* project. The burden is not on you to come up with the right words to say to convince your son or daughter that Jesus is truly God come to earth to save us from our sins. The power is not in you; the power is in the gospel. Don't be ashamed of it.

Earlier I told you the story about my father's miraculous conversion. One of my favorite parts of the story happened about two weeks before he trusted Christ alone for his salvation. I was away at a conference, and Amy encouraged our kids to make cards and send them to "Papa Bill." Amy didn't tell them what to say, and because I was away I was unaware the cards were even sent. My daughter Lissy, who was nine at the time, made a card, and on the cover she wrote, "Heaven rocks!" Inside she wrote, "For God so loved the world that He gave His one and only Son, that whoever believes in Him might not perish but have everlasting life—John 3:16." My son RW, who was eleven, wrote these words in his card: "Papa Bill, We are praying for you. 'For all have sinned and fallen short of the glory of God.'—Romans 3:23. I hope you enjoy this verse. Love, RW." This is *exactly* what he wrote! I imagine if I'd been there, I would have provided some editorial assistance to smooth some of the rough edges. Instead, the cards were mailed with the exact words each child wanted to express.

My mother, Angie, and stepfather, Jack, visited my father in the hospital on August 10. My father asked them a strange question: "Is there anything I can do for you?" Jack responded, "Yes, Bill. You can trust Christ. We want to be in heaven with you." My father pointed over to four construction-paper cards taped to his window... the cards sent to him from my children. He said, "I've been thinking a lot about that lately. Let me see those cards." He, together with my mother and Jack, read the Scriptures written with the crayons and markers. My mom then shared the gospel with him. He had heard these Scriptures many times in his life. But this was the night he responded with repentance and belief. God's Word is true! These cards were not creative, except for the great artwork. My kids were not ashamed of the gospel—for the gospel is the power of God unto salvation.

TAKE A RISK

Choosing to initiate meaningful conversations with your son or daughter is a great risk. If you go to your child and repent for mistakes you've made, he or she may not be willing to forgive you. If you humbly seek to draw the heart of your son or daughter to yours, you child may pull farther away. These conversations are difficult, awkward, and risky. You have no idea what the reaction will be. Your attempt to express concern to your child about his or her spiritual life may, in fact, seem to make things worse... at least on the surface. But here we must all ask ourselves, "What is the alternative? Giving up? Saying nothing?

Not trying to do all in our power to help our children get safely home to their Father in heaven?"

I prayed for my father to come to Christ for more than thirty years. I looked for opportunities to talk with him about spiritual things. One morning, when he was about eighty years old, we went to breakfast. I got up the nerve to try again and I said, "Dad, it wouldn't surprise me if you were angry with God for allowing your mother to die as soon as you were born." The sentence was barely out of my mouth, and a tear rolled down his cheek. He quickly wiped it away and said, "Let's not talk about that." It was a vivid illustration to me of how my father, and many like him, can appear so spiritually hard but in reality are paper-thin. Sometimes a single sentence, thought, or sentiment breaks through.

Through the next decade my father made it very clear to me that he didn't want to talk about spiritual things with me. A year before he died, he laid it out for me in no uncertain terms. He wasn't rude with me but made his wishes perfectly clear that he didn't want to hear any more religious stuff from me or my family.

Embracing the mission to encourage faith in your wayward child is perilous. But the soul of your son or daughter is worth every risk, and desperate times call for desperate measures. One of my prayers, as you have taken the journey through this book, is that God will fill your heart with eagerness, passion, and courage. I want us all to have an appropriate *desperation* to see all our children saved, walking with the Lord, and spending eternity in heaven together.

SHARE YOUR STORIES OF REPENTANCE AND SPIRITUAL GROWTH

One way to start a spiritual conversation with your son or daughter is to share with him or her things that God is doing in your life to shape and grow your character. Rather than focus the conversation on a character issue in your *child's* life, start a conversation about a character issue in *your* life. It might sound something like this:

Son, you know how I have some bad driving habits. I was driving home from work the other day and this guy cut me off coming off the exit ramp. God must be really working on me, because I stayed calm. I didn't curse under my breath. I only gave a light honk of the horn. I wanted to really lay on it, believe me! I was encouraged that God is not through with me yet.

This approach enables you to bring up spiritual issues in a way that has nothing directly to do with your child. This approach is a far cry from, "I'm concerned about your spiritual life. Did you go to church this week?" Each of us can start a spiritual conversation by simply being open, honest, and humble about how God is shaping our own character. Our children are fairly well versed in the subject of our character problems. When we're humble about our growth areas it often has the effect of softening the hearts of our children.

USE LETTERS TO OPEN SPIRITUAL CONVERSATIONS

You can use letters to open spiritual conversations. Some of you are thinking, *This is ridiculous. There's no way in the world my child is going to write a letter to me!* For some of you that may be true, but others of you have children who enjoy writing either traditional letters or e-mails. I've counseled many young adults who have a terrible time expressing their thoughts and feelings face-to-face, but when they're in front of a keyboard, they open up. E-mail, texting, or online social networks are not, of course, a substitute for authentic human relationships. Some of our children and grandchildren are relationally stunted as a result of too much technology. Communicating via letters or e-mail may, however, be a positive first step in opening up important conversations.

Writing letters or e-mails to our children can be a powerful way to encourage them. I was blessed and encouraged by Greg Vaughn's book, *Letters from Dad*.[3] Greg had never been close to his father. After his father died, Greg was cleaning out his own garage. He was grieving that the only thing he had to remember his father by was an old tackle box. He didn't even have his father's signature. His thoughts quickly turned to his own children and he thought, *If I were to die today, what would my children have in their hands to let them know that I loved them and that they were the treasure of my life?* He concluded that if he died that moment, his children would be in the same position he was in, aching for something to hold that told them they were loved. In *Letters from Dad*, Greg teaches fathers (the principles work great for moms too) how to write letters of encouragement and blessing to their wives and children.

After reading *Letters from Dad*, I decided to take action. I wrote a letter to my wife and to each of my children, expressing my love for them, blessing them, and thanking God for them. I have given them additional letters as the years have gone by, but not as many as I should. About six months after I gave the first letter to my son RW, I was spending time with him in his room and noticed the letter sitting on the floor in the corner of his room. He was playing with Legos and we were talking about random things. When I saw the letter on the floor, I couldn't help but feel a little hurt. I'd taken the time to give him something special. It was on good paper, and I gave it to him in a good envelope. My special letter was now wrinkled and laying haphazardly on the floor. I awkwardly said, "RW,... I see that the letter I gave you is over there on the floor... Do you ever... take it out and read it?"

He didn't look up from playing with his Legos but quickly replied, "Every day, Dad. I read it every day."

I was stunned. I'm not sure how long I sat there trying to take in what my son had just said. Hesitantly I said, "Every day?... You really... read it every day?"

"Yup."

The reason the letter was all wrinkled was because it was getting heavy use! I would much rather the letter be read every day than sit in pristine condition in its original envelope, far from my son's heart and mind.

I encourage you to take a bold step and write a letter of encouragement to your son or daughter.[4] A letter is a marvelous way to express unconditional love. It is God's desire for our children to experience uncon- ditional love from us, so that their hearts will be prepared to experience unconditional love from Him. If you choose to write a letter of encouragement, give your child more than performance-based affirmation. How often do

> A letter is a marvel- ous way to express unconditional love.

we tell our children that we're proud of them apart from any- thing they've done? How frequently do we tell our children we love them "just because"? One of the questions that I routinely ask young adults in counseling sessions is, "Do you feel as if your parents love you more when you do right, and love you less when you mess up?" The majority say yes. In short, they feel that their parents love them *conditionally.* Our children need to hear powerful words and phrases like these:

"I love you no matter what."

"I'm proud of you just because you are you."

"I'll always love you no matter what you do."

"There's nothing you can do to make me love you any less, and there's nothing you can do that will make me love you any more."

"I believe in you."

"I'm praying for you."

"I'm committed to you for the rest of your life."

"I'll never turn my back on you."

I recommend keeping your encouragement letters to a single page. Better to send three single-page letters over the course of a few months than one long letter. Letters provide a permanent record of our thoughts and feelings toward our children. Letters are powerful, and therefore must be used carefully. Letters are not the way to express criticism or disappointment. Those sen- timents will then be permanently recorded and do more harm than good. This is not to say that it's inappropriate for parents to express concerns, criticisms, anger, or disappointment. Rather, those matters are better handled face-to-face, or if that's logisti-cally impossible, on the phone. We'll talk more about how to handle these sensitive issues in the pages ahead.

Letters can also be used to open a conversation about spiritual matters. Again, this approach will not work for every relation-ship, but sending a letter may crack open a door. Consider writ-ing a letter or e-mail to your child that goes something like this:

Dear _____,

I realize it's a little strange to get a letter from me, but I had an idea that I wanted to run past you. You may not be interested in this, so I want you to feel free to say no.

Over the years we've had some conversations about spiri-tual things. I imagine that at times you've felt I was being too pushy, and perhaps at other times that I didn't share my heart enough. Regardless of the past, I want to do everything I can do to build a closer relationship with you. Most of all, I want to be able to talk with you about things that matter. I want you to be able to share your heart with me, and I want to be able to share my heart with you. I realize we may not agree on everything, and that's okay.

Here's my idea. I would like you to consider writing letters back and forth to each other. They don't have to be long. I realize you're busy. But it would mean the world to me if we could share our questions, beliefs, and convictions with each other. You have told me in the past that you don't see things the way I do when it comes to faith. I'd like to hear more from you about that. Perhaps you could write down some of your thoughts and feelings about religious matters, and then I'd have the chance to respond. The purpose is not to debate or argue, but to share our hearts with each other. I thought that I might go first and write a short letter to you about some of the struggles I've had with faith in God over the years. You could then respond however you wanted to. What do you think? You can either write back with your response, or just

talk to me. The bottom line is that I love you and I want to have a better relationship with you.

Sending a letter like this is risky… but your child's soul is worth the risk. Consider having a friend or spouse read your letter before you send it. It's easy to express criticism without even knowing it. A third party can help spot words and phrases that may hurt rather than heal.

READ AND DISCUSS A BOOK TOGETHER

Many of you have a cordial relationship with your son or daughter. You share meals together. Your child pleasantly participates in family gatherings. You talk together about sports, travel, jobs, and the grandkids. But the relationship is a mile wide and only an inch deep. If people observed how you relate to each other they would conclude that things were great between you. But you know better. While you enjoy the day-to-day friendship you have with your child, conversations never get past the superficial. You and your child have a day-to-day friendship stuck in day-to-day conversations. What can you do to nudge the relationship to a deeper level? Consider reading and discussing a book together.

As with the suggestion above to write letters, some of you are already looking ahead to the next section. I can hear you now: "My kid hasn't read a book in twenty years, and he certainly isn't going to start by reading one with me!" Others of you have children who are voracious readers. What if your child's interest in reading could spark more meaningful conversations? Some of you have tried this before and the results were less than desirable. Many parents, though, instead of giving a lecture, give their kids books to read. They hope that if the lecture comes from someone else their child will listen. Our kids are pretty smart and they usually see this one coming a mile away. How many times have we tried, "I came across this book the other day, and I thought you might be interested in it." That's a lie. We *know* that they're not going to be *interested*. We're praying for a miracle and that they'll crack the binding! Here's a better way to try this idea:

> I've been thinking about something. I appreciate the fact that we have a good relationship. I know there are a lot of families that can't stand to be together. I also appreciate the fact that we can talk together. I enjoy our conversations. Now you may not be interested in this idea, but I want to share it with you anyway. If you don't like it, just tell me. No problem. I'd like to be able to talk with you about important things. We talk about day-to-day life, but I sometimes feel we could go deeper. I had a crazy idea for how we might do this. I know you like to read. What if we read the same book together and then talked about what we're reading? I don't want this to be burdensome. We just read the same book, and then whenever we can, we share our thoughts with each other. I think we could have some great conversations and it would deepen our relationship. I realize we won't agree on everything, but agreeing isn't the point. If you're game to try this, I'd love it if you'd choose the first book. You can pick whatever you want.[5] My hope is that our reading the book together would help us talk about new things in a new way. What do you think?

Let's imagine that your son or daughter chose to go down this path with you and issues of faith begin to arise in your future conversations. Many of you may hear your child express something to you along these lines:

> I understand that this Christian stuff is good for you and that it works for you. I just think that there are all sorts of different ways to go through life. There are a bunch of different religions that all basically teach the same things. As long as you're a good person, that's what counts.

Everything in you will immediately want to try and persuade them about why their perspective isn't true. You're not wrong to do this. In the next section we'll talk about the need to speak truth to our children, even if they don't necessarily want to hear it. Disagreement or persuasion, however, may not be the best *first* response. In the spirit of our earlier parenting principles, consider responding like this:

> Thanks for sharing your thoughts with me. I appreciate your honesty. I'd like to hear more along the lines of what you just said. Can you tell me why you've come to believe these things?

The final question above is an important one to use if you're able to have spiritual conversations with your child. People often make grand proclamations about their convictions or beliefs. Sometimes the proclamations are serious and other times they're used to get a rise out of us. When we gently and respectfully ask, "Why do you believe that?" or, "Where did you develop that conviction?" we're guiding the conversation to an important place. Be gentle. Remind yourself of the third principle: *draw your child's heart to yours.* Many people, when asked, "Why do you believe that?" or "How did you come to that conviction?" will say, "I don't know, that's just the way I think." If that's the response you get, just nod your head, and move the conversation forward. Allow the Holy Spirit to convict and convince your son or daughter that his or her beliefs are based on *themselves* rather than on the solid ground of God and His Word.

SPEAK WITH GRACE AND TRUTH

Speaking with grace and truth is one of the most important and most difficult parts in the mission of pointing our children's hearts to Christ. The best way to grow as a godly parent is to learn from Father God. He is a perfect father, and we are His wayward children. Throughout the Scriptures, God comes to His children with both justice and love. Is God more *just* or is He more *loving*? Theologically, the question makes no sense. God is completely just and completely loving at the same time. God deals with us in judgment and mercy. Is He more judgmental or more merciful? Again, the premise of the question is flawed. God is full of judgment and full of mercy all the time. This paradox is expressed perfectly in God the Son, Jesus Christ. Consider how the apostle John speaks of Jesus: "The Word became flesh and made his dwelling among us. We have seen his glory, the glory of the One and Only, who came from the Father, full of grace and truth" (John 1:14).

Jesus came *full of grace and truth.* These are two things that rarely go together. Is Jesus all about *truth* or is He all about *grace*? He is all about truth *and* all about grace. When Jesus spoke, the volume on truth was all the way up. In those exact moments, the volume on grace was all the way up as well.

Parenting with truth and grace starts early. Recently, a mother of two preschoolers asked me, "How can I discipline my kids in a way that will never make them feel like they're a bad person?" She was more than a little shocked when I explained to her that our goal is not to ensure that our kids never feel bad about themselves. If our children never come to realize that they're inherently sinful, they won't ever repent, believe in Christ, and be saved. If parents speak this truth to their children, is it harsh, graceless, or unloving? If it's done with a condescending and shaming tone, then yes. If it's done with a heartfelt, tender, compassionate tone, then it is a very loving thing to say. If we don't tell our children plainly about the reality of sin and judgment, that is unloving.

> Shielding our children from the only true message of salvation is perhaps the most unloving thing we could do.

We believe that God has revealed the truth about heaven, hell, and eternity. We believe that our children will one day stand before their Creator and give an account. We believe that God made only one way for us to be saved from hell and saved for heaven—to repent of our sin and believe in Jesus Christ alone. The only way to be saved is to trust in Jesus Christ's death and

A few days later your child comes back to you and says, "I've been thinking about your question. I couldn't come up with much of anything. I suppose you can pray for me. That wouldn't drive me nuts." Thank your child for getting back to you, and then a few days later ask him or her in person, on the phone, or via e-mail, "How can I be praying for you this week?" If your son or daughter seems annoyed at the question, you can say, "I'm sorry. I didn't mean to upset you. A few days ago you said that one of the things that I could do was to pray for you, so I wanted to follow through on what you said. If this is irritating for you, give me something else I could be doing that would be better."

Did you know you can ask spiritually wayward children to pray for you? It may seem strange, but it can have a powerful impact.

> I'm going to be getting together with your grandma next week. You know that your grandma and I have had a hard time in our relationship over the years. This may sound strange to you, but it would sure mean a lot to me if you could say a couple of prayers for me while I'm meeting with her. It would really help me. Would you be willing to do that?

You might be surprised how readily your son or daughter accepts your request. Asking for prayer invites your child into your spiritual life in a way that is not critical or confrontational. With this approach, you're simply trying to involve your son or daughter in things that are important to you.

We've explored different ways to practice this final principle of pointing your child's heart to Christ. I wish there was a magic formula, a step-by-step process, or perfect words that I could give that would soften your child's heart and bring him or her to repentance and salvation. We come back to the truth that the power to point your child's heart to Christ rests with God and His Word. In the next and final chapter we'll turn to God's Word for the encouragement we need in the present, and the hopeful vision we need for the future.

Questions for Reflection/Discussion

1. Do you tend to lean more toward truth or grace in your relationship with your child?
2. What is a specific thing you can do to turn up the volume on the weak side?
3. If your son or daughter came to you and asked you to explain the message of the Bible, would you be ready to give an answer? If you answered no to this question, what can you do to prepare yourself?[6]
4. Which action step in this chapter might God be calling you to practice?

Chapter 10

FOR GENERATIONS TO COME

As you've been reading this book, your thoughts have been on one or more of your children. But encouraging faith in our own children is only the first step in the amazing multigenerational impact to which God calls us. Consider this multigenerational vision as described in Psalm 78:1–7:

> O my people, hear my teaching;
> listen to the words of my mouth.
> I will open my mouth in parables,
> I will utter hidden things, things from of old—
> what we have heard and known,
> what our fathers have told us.
> We will not hide them from their children;
> we will tell the next generation
> the praiseworthy deeds of the Lord,
> his power, and the wonders he has done.
> He decreed statutes for Jacob
> and established the law in Israel,
> which he commanded our forefathers
> to teach their children,
> so the next generation would know them,
> even the children yet to be born,
> and they in turn would tell their children.

Then they would put their trust in God
and would not forget his deeds
but would keep his commands.

The writer says, "I will utter hidden things, things from of old—
what we have heard and known, what our fathers have told us"
(vv. 2–3). My father didn't tell me about the Lord. Regardless of
what kind of family we came from, whether or not our parents
passed faith to us, God calls us to share the psalmist's declaration: "We will not hide them from their children; we will tell the
next generation the praiseworthy deeds of the LORD, his power,
and the wonders he has done" (v. 4).

God has graciously brought you into a relationship with Him
through Jesus Christ. He has put His Word, the Bible, in your
hands and enabled you through the Holy Spirit to understand
and believe the truth of the gospel. God calls His children to
make it their mission to tell the next generation the praiseworthy
deeds of the Lord. God gets tremendous glory when parents
and grandparents tell their children and grandchildren of the
wonders He has done. Why are we called to this? "So the next
generation would know them, even the children yet to be born"
(v. 6). We all want our children to love God, serve Him, and
arrive safely home in heaven. But that's not all. God has created
us to influence and bless not only our children, but our grandchildren, great-grandchildren, and beyond.

God wants our hearts turned not only to our children, but
to *the children yet to be born*. God is already thinking of those
boys and girls, men and women. Are you? My prayer is that, as
you embrace this mission to encourage faith in your adult child,
you'll also be thinking of grandchildren and great-grandchildren
yet to be born. God already has plans for their lives—that *they
in turn would tell their children*. This psalm is all about embracing a multigenerational vision for our lives and ministry. God
desires for you to pass the baton of faith to your children, who
will pass it to their children, generation after generation until
Christ returns.

resurrection on our behalf. How can we as parents believe these things and not speak of them passionately to our own children? Are we afraid of being unloving? Shielding our children from the only true message of salvation is perhaps the most unloving thing we could do.

Jesus is full of grace and truth. We are usually better at one, and not so comfortable with the other. Think of each person in your family. Is he or she more graceful or more truthful? Is that person more likely to be *kind* or to be *right*? If I were to ask your children whether you leaned on the grace-side or the truth-side, what would they say? What would you say?

Truth and grace are not mutually exclusive.

If you're going to embrace this mission of encouraging faith in your adult children, you must commit yourselves to turning the volume all the way up in truth *and* grace. Truth and grace are not mutually exclusive. As we think about how to respond to situations, we can agonize, *Either I need to tell the truth, or be graceful and let it go*; we think and act as if grace and truth are inherently in conflict with one another. But is it really possible to have grace without truth?

Only in two other places in the New Testament, outside of the gospel of John, are grace and truth found together. One is Colossians 1:6: "All over the world this gospel is bearing fruit and growing, just as it has been doing among you since the day you heard it and understood God's grace in all its truth." Look at the last phrase, *God's grace in all its truth*. It doesn't say, "God's grace in spite of the truth" or "God's grace in contrast to the truth." According to this passage, grace possesses truth. They can't be separated. The apostle John brings grace and truth together again in one of his letters: "Grace, mercy and peace from God the Father and from Jesus Christ, the Father's Son, will be with us in truth and love" (2 John 1:3).

What is grace's relationship with truth? God says here that grace, mercy, and peace reside in truth and love. Consider God's love for us as our heavenly Father. Can we separate God's grace from His truth? God speaks to us in the Scriptures and tells us that He made us for His glory. We chose to sin, and that sin deserves death. He chose to become a human being in Jesus Christ and take our sins upon Himself on the cross. He conquered death through His resurrection and now makes forgiveness and salvation available to us by His grace through faith. Because these things are *true*, God offers us His *grace*. Because God offers us *grace*, these things are *true*.

There is no true grace without truth, but can there be truth without grace? This second one seems more plausible, doesn't it? You may have someone in your life right now, and you'd love to give that person a big helping of uncensored truth. But when we unload on others, are we being totally truthful? Are we really giving them the whole picture, the picture that God sees?

When we confront our children in anger about the things that need to change in their lives, are we truthful? Do we have logs in our own eyes while we tell our children about the specks in theirs? Do we include the truth that our sons and daughters are unique and priceless creations of God? Do we mention that Jesus went to the cross to pay for not only their sins, but that He paid for ours as well? Those are inconvenient truths in the moment of confrontation. So do we omit them and unleash the part of the truth that we want to? But part of the truth isn't the truth. Full grace and full truth are always found together. It's gracious to speak the truth to our children. It's truthful to speak grace to our children. God calls us to be full of grace and full of truth. What can we do in our relationships with our sons or daughter to turn up the volume of grace in our relationships? What can we do to turn up the volume of truth?

A friend of mine faced a traumatic situation with his adult son. The son was far from God and pursuing a selfish divorce, thereby bringing terrible pain upon his wife and children. What does a father do when he sees his son making destructive decisions? My friend came to his son, full of grace and truth. As you read the following words he shared with his son, look for high-volume grace and high-volume truth.

> Son, I want you to know that I love you very much. I want my words to bring you hope. As you've grown into manhood, I've watched you make some mistakes without interfering. But I can't stay silent as you proceed with your divorce. I need to share my heart with you and remind you of what God has said. I know that you've been hurt in your marriage. The pain runs very deep. But you're not without hope. This hurt can be healed. God wants to work a miracle in your life and family. The question is, will you let Him do it?
>
> Consider this image. Take two pieces of paper and glue them together. Allow the paper to remain together for over a decade. Then, try to pull them apart. If you tried to do this, both the single sheets of paper would be seriously damaged. You and your wife will suffer untold pain if you continue down your present path. I know that you've used alcohol to deal with your pain in the past. Why not turn to God?
>
> I want to be clear with you that divorcing your wife in this situation is wrong. In the Bible, God does grant permission for divorce in certain circumstances. Those are not your circumstances. God does not want you to do this. I don't want you to do this. God speaks about divorce in Malachi 2:16 where it says, "'For I hate divorce,' says the Lord God of Israel."
>
> You're free to make your own choices. I won't stop loving you if you choose to do this. But this decision will cause trauma and pain that can never be undone. I'm here to help you. I know the road to reconciliation will be long and hard. Let's walk the road together.

This is an example of one father who did his best to be full of grace and truth with his son. Have you given more truth or have you given more grace over the years? Which do you need to focus on in order to be full of both?

ASK YOUR CHILD TO HELP YOU

Trying to talk about anything spiritual with your child can be a struggle. All the ideas we're talking about are risky. We're afraid of how our children will respond, and often rightly so. If we start with the "Jesus talk," their eyes start to glaze over. Did you know that you can ask your son or daughter to help you? Consider sharing this with your adult child:

> _____, I want to talk with you about something that's been on my mind. It's uncomfortable for me to talk about, so I may seem nervous. As you know I sometimes try to talk with you about faith and spiritual things. I know that's not always comfortable for you. In fact, sometimes you bristle a bit. You know that I believe that God wants me to do all I can to encourage faith in you, but I feel as if the way I'm going about it isn't working very well. When I try to talk about Christ or the Bible, sometimes you get upset. I don't usually respond well to that, which only makes matters worse. All this is to say, I'm here to ask for your help. I'd like to ask you a question, and you don't need to answer right now. If you get back to me in a couple days that would be fine. Here's my question: Can you please give me three suggestions for how I can be obedient to God in seeking to encourage you spiritually, but will not drive you nuts?

"Sure! I'll give you something you can do! You can leave me alone and stop talking to me about all this religious hocus pocus."

> I'm so sorry, _____. That's about the only suggestion that I can't do. I know you think this is crazy, but I believe this is something God wants me to do, so I can't just sit back and do nothing. So what do you think I can do? Please think about it. Otherwise I'll keep trying my own ideas, and I think we can both agree that my ideas haven't been working so well.

In the beginning you laid the foundations of the earth,
and the heavens are the work of your hands.
They will perish, but you remain;
they will all wear out like a garment.
Like clothing you will change them
and they will be discarded.
But you remain the same,
and your years will never end.
The children of your servants will live in your presence;
their descendants will be established before you.

Here is how you might pray this psalm back to God; "Dear God, in the beginning You laid the foundations of the earth, and the heavens are the work of Your hands. I praise You for Your great power! The heavens and earth will perish, but You remain; they will all wear out like a garment. Like clothing You will change them and they will be discarded. Thank You God that You never change. You never wear out. Your years will never end. I am Your servant and I praise You. I pray that the children of Your servant will live in Your presence. May my children's children be established before You."

It is through prayer that we engage in spiritual battle for the souls of our children. Isaiah 49:25 is a Scripture that can guide in "battle prayer":

But this is what the LORD says: "Yes, captives will be taken from warriors, and plunder retrieved from the fierce; I will contend with those who contend with you, and your children I will save."

Here is how you might pray this Scripture. "Dear Lord, I am here to do battle for the soul of my child. _____ is a captive to this world. Your Word says that You have the power to rescue captives from fierce warriors. Please rescue _____! I ask that You will work against those who seek to do harm to my child. Remove everything that is hindering _____ from giving his/her heart to me and to You. Your Word says, 'Your children I will save.' I come before Your throne boldly, and I ask You to save my child."

CONCLUSION

Isaiah 59 and 60 give us a terrible picture of our sinful world, and a marvelous picture of God's grace and plan for salvation. Chapter 59 begins with a tragic and bleak, but accurate view of the world apart from Christ:

> Surely the arm of the LORD is not too short to save, nor his ear too dull to hear. But your iniquities have separated you from your God; your sins have hidden his face from you, so that he will not hear....
>
> Their feet rush into sin; they are swift to shed innocent blood. Their thoughts are evil thoughts; ruin and destruction mark their ways. The way of peace they do not know; there is no justice in their paths. They have turned them into crooked roads; no one who walks in them will know peace. So justice is far from us, and righteousness does not reach us. We look for light, but all is darkness; for brightness, but we walk in deep shadows....
>
> For our offenses are many in your sight, and our sins testify against us. Our offenses are ever with us, and we acknowledge our iniquities: rebellion and treachery against the LORD, turning our backs on our God, fomenting oppression and revolt, uttering lies our hearts have conceived. So justice is driven back, and righteousness stands at a distance; truth has stumbled in the streets, honesty cannot enter. Truth is nowhere to be found, and whoever shuns evil becomes a prey. The LORD looked and was displeased that there was no justice. (vv. 1–2, 7–9, 12–15)

The picture keeps getting worse and worse. The world is filled with pain, rebellion, misery, and loneliness. Our families can be filled with those things, too. What can possibly be done? Is there any hope for our families and for our wayward children?

> He saw that there was no one, he was appalled that there was
> no one to intervene; so his own arm worked salvation for him,
> and his own righteousness sustained him.... "The Redeemer
> will come to Zion, to those in Jacob who repent of their sins,"
> declares the LORD.
> "As for me, this is my covenant with them," says the LORD. "My
> Spirit, who is on you, and my words that I have put in your
> mouth will not depart from your mouth, or from the mouths
> of your children, or from the mouths of their descendants from
> this time on and forever," says the LORD. (vv. 16, 20–21)

Praise the Lord! God has the power to turn the heart of your son or daughter back to Him. God delights in bringing prodigals home. Generational faithfulness is His joy. He graciously puts His Word in our mouths, so that it might come from the mouths of our children, and their children, and their children, until the Lord returns.

As if this vision of salvation was not enough, the next chapter of Isaiah begins with a vision of the Messiah and the work He will accomplish:

> "Arise, shine, for your light has come, and the glory of the
> LORD rises upon you. See, darkness covers the earth and thick
> darkness is over the peoples, but the LORD rises upon you and
> his glory appears over you. Nations will come to your light,
> and kings to the brightness of your dawn. Lift up your eyes
> and look about you: All assemble and come to you; your sons
> come from afar, and your daughters are carried on the arm.
> Then you will look and be radiant, your heart will throb and
> swell with joy." (60:1–5)

Pray that God will show His glory to your children. Pray that God will transform your life and character so that you shine like the dawn for your children. Like the father in the parable of the lost son, lift up your eyes. Scan the horizon. May God give you the joy of seeing *your sons come from afar, and your daughters carried on the arm. Then you will look and be radiant, your heart will throb and swell with joy!*

I pray that God has used your study of this book to motivate you into acting upon the four biblical parenting principles. The principles are not the sort of things we put on a list, check off, and put in the past. Rather, God calls us as parents to continually commit ourselves to

- offer our hearts to Him.
- turn our hearts to our children.
- draw our children's hearts to ours.
- point our children's hearts to Christ.

As you seek to act on these principles each day, remember to hold fast to the goal:

Our children loving God with all of their hearts, putting their full faith and trust in Jesus for their present and their future, and arriving safely home together with us in heaven.

Amen!

What happens when parents and grandparents make it their mission to encourage faith in their children, rather than delegating that mission to the church or hoping someone else will do it? This psalm says that "then they would put their trust in God and would not forget his deeds, but would keep his commands" (v. 7).

FROM YOUR FAMILY TO THE WORLD

When we encourage faith in our children, we have an impact for Christ on the world. If, by God's grace, your child follows Christ, everyone in his or her circle of influence will be blessed. Consider the words of the apostle Peter in Acts 2. Here, Jesus has ascended to heaven, the Holy Spirit has come up on the followers of Jesus, and Peter is preaching the gospel to the crowds. This is his final call:

> Repent and be baptized, every one of you, in the name of Jesus Christ for the forgiveness of your sins. And you will receive the gift of the Holy Spirit. The promise is for you and your children and for all who are far off—for all whom the Lord our God will call. (Acts 2:38–39)

In this passage we find the "order" by which the good news is to be spread. The first implied question is, will you respond to God's grace and trust Christ? *The promise is for you.* The second question is, will your children also trust Christ? When we think of ministry or evangelism, we must think of the souls of our children first.

When we think of ministry or evangelism, we must think of the souls of our children first.

Then, together with our children, God gives us the opportunity to take the gospel beyond our family to *all who are far off.* Do you have a heart to reach your neighbors and to see the gospel taken to the ends of the earth? Then do all in your power to encourage faith in your children and grandchildren. Encouraging faith in your adult child advances the kingdom of God.

One of my favorite quotes comes from William Bradford, who led the Pilgrims across the Atlantic on the *Mayflower*. In his journal, *Of Plymouth Plantation*, he explained the mission that drove them to relocate their church from Holland to the New World: "We cherish a great hope, and an inward zeal, of laying good foundations for the advance of the Gospel of the Kingdom of Christ to the remote parts of the earth, even if we should be but stepping-stones to others in the performance of so great a work."[1]

In my family, we often use this purpose statement to talk about the mission that God has given to us. Amy and I may not bring the gospel to the remote parts of the earth, but we believe the multitude of our descendents will. Do you have a heart for global missions? Encourage faith in your children, and the gospel will multiply. Do you feel called to ministries of compassion, justice, and mercy? Encourage faith in your children, and compassion will increase in the world for generations to come.

NEVER TOO LATE

It's never too late for God to use you to launch a multigenerational movement of faith in your family. It may be that you came to Christ as an adult, and that your life before conversion was disastrous. Perhaps your wayward child remembers those days and still finds it difficult to believe that God has truly changed you. Consider the dramatic story of Manasseh in the Scriptures:

> Manasseh was twelve years old when he became king, and he reigned in Jerusalem fifty-five years. He did evil in the eyes of the LORD, following the detestable practices of the nations the LORD had driven out before the Israelites. He rebuilt the high places his father Hezekiah had demolished; he also erected altars to the Baals and made Asherah poles. He bowed down to all the starry hosts and worshiped them. He built altars in the temple of the LORD, of which the LORD had said, "My Name will remain in Jerusalem forever." In both courts of the temple of the LORD, he built altars to all

the starry hosts. He sacrificed his sons in the fire in the Valley of Ben Hinnom, practiced sorcery, divination and witchcraft, and consulted mediums and spiritists. He did much evil in the eyes of the LORD, provoking him to anger. (2 Chron. 33:1–6)

Manasseh was one of the most wicked kings in the history of Israel. He worshipped idols and led the people to do the same. He threw his own children into pits of fire, sacrificing them to his demonic gods. God did not let this evil go unpunished.

The LORD spoke to Manasseh and his people, but they paid no attention. So the LORD brought against them the army commanders of the king of Assyria, who took Manasseh prisoner, put a hook in his nose, bound him with bronze shackles and took him to Babylon. In his distress he sought the favor of the LORD his God and humbled himself greatly before the God of his fathers. And when he prayed to him, the LORD was moved by his entreaty and listened to his plea; so he brought him back to Jerusalem and to his kingdom. Then Manasseh knew that the LORD is God.... He got rid of the foreign gods and removed the image from the temple of the LORD, as well as all the altars he had built on the temple hill and in Jerusalem; and he threw them out of the city. Then he restored the altar of the LORD and sacrificed fellowship offerings and thank offerings on it, and told Judah to serve the LORD, the God of Israel. (2 Chron. 33:10–13; 15–16)

Manasseh repented! For the last five years of his life, he was a man on a mission. He tore down all the pagan altars he had built and raised up the altar of the Lord that he had torn down. He called the people to repent just as he had done, and to serve the Lord. Have you committed terrible sins in your life? Consider Manasseh, his sins, his repentance, and God's forgiveness.

It's possible that the person most dramatically affected by Manasseh's repentance and radical pursuit of pleasing God was his grandson, Josiah. Josiah was only one year old when his grandfather turned from sin. From age one to six Josiah saw his grandfather worshipping God, tearing down places of idol worship, raising up the altar of the Lord, and pleading with the people to follow God and God alone. It's reasonable to believe that Josiah heard some stories about the man his grandfather used to be, but all Josiah knew was, *regardless of the past*, his grandfather loved God *now*. Josiah needed that example from Manasseh, because he would become king at the tender age of eight.

> Josiah was eight years old when he became king, and he reigned in Jerusalem thirty-one years. He did what was right in the eyes of the Lord and walked in the ways of his father David, not turning aside to the right or to the left.... In his twelfth year he began to purge Judah and Jerusalem of high places, Asherah poles, carved idols and cast images. Under his direction the altars of the Baals were torn down; he cut to pieces the incense altars that were above them, and smashed the Asherah poles, the idols and the images. (2 Chron. 34:1–4)

Manasseh's repentance blessed his grandson Josiah, and Josiah continued his grandfather's mission to call the people of Israel back to God. Josiah became one of the most godly and important kings in the history of Israel. Your choice to pursue God and walk humbly with Him will have a ripple effect in your family for generations to come.

WITH GOD ALL THINGS ARE POSSIBLE

Only God has the power to bring about this glorious multi-generational vision. Therefore, the foundation of our work as parents is in prayer. One of the best ways we can pray is by offering God's Word back to Him. The Scriptures help us praise God, adore God, and plead with Him for the right things. I encourage you to begin the habit of praying for your adult child, using Psalm 102:25–28:

3. J. J. Heller, "Love Me," *Only Love Remains*, produced by Mitch Dane, distributed by Stone Table Records, 2006. Printed with permission.

Chapter 6
THE FREEDOM OF FORGIVENESS

1. "Interesting Tree Facts," United Nations Environment Programme, http://www.unep.org/Documents.Multilingual /Default.asp?DocumentID=445&ArticleID=4852&l=en.
2. Hear the entire story of my father's miraculous conversion at www.visionaryparenting.com/audiodownloads.htm, "Do You Not Know? A Miracle Story of God's Faithfulness," August 31, 2008.

Chapter 7
DRAW YOUR CHILD'S HEART TO YOURS

1. Two excellent books on this subject are David A. Black, *The Myth of Adolescence* (Yorba Linda, CA: Davidson, 1999); and Alex Harris and Brett Harris, *Do Hard Things* (Colorado Springs, CO: Multnomah, 2008).
2. There are, of course, situations in which teens are in dangerous and abusive situations and church leaders may appropriately need to seek to protect children from danger.
3. I'm not saying that it's not natural and healthy for our children to develop increasingly independent lives as they become adults. Rather, as they become increasingly independent functionally, God desires that we remain close to our children spiritually. Eventually, God wants our children to have their own households, and even though we as a family might be spread out around the world, God desires for all the generations in the family to maintain a lifelong, Christ-centered heart-connection with one another.
4. John G. Paton, *John G. Paton: Missionary to the New Hebrides, An Autobiography Edited by His Brother* (1889; repr., Edinburgh: The Banner of Truth Trust, 1965), 25–26.
5. Your younger children may still be teenagers. Consider taking a powerful thirty-day journey to build your heart-connection

with them: Dr. Richard Ross and Dr. Gus Reyes, *30 Days: Turning the Hearts of Parents and Teenagers Toward Each Other* (Nashville: Lifeway, 2003), http://josiahpress.com/index.htm.

Chapter 8
REBUILDING THE BRIDGE

1. Emerson Eggerich, *Love and Respect* (Nashville: Thomas Nelson, 2004).

Chapter 9
POINT YOUR CHILD'S HEART TO CHRIST

1. By no means is this intended to be an exhaustive treatment of the parenting principles that God gives to us in the Scriptures.
2. Abraham Piper, "Twelve Ways to Love Your Wayward Child," May 9, 2007, Desiring God, http://www.desiringgod.org/resource-library/resources/12-ways-to-love-your-wayward-child.
3. Greg Vaughn, *Letters from Dad* (Nashville: Thomas Nelson, 2005).
4. Earlier in the book, I encouraged you to avoid using letters when asking your children for forgiveness. On the other hand, letters are an excellent tool for expressing affirmation and encouragement.
5. In the unlikely event that your child chooses a book that is particularly evil, profane, or graphic, don't hesitate to respectfully ask for a different suggestion.
6. Consider learning these five Scriptures from the book of Romans which could help you explain the message of salvation to your child. Romans 1:18–20 teaches that God created the world and that because of the evidence of creation we have no excuse not to believe in Him. Romans 3:23 teaches that everyone is guilty of sinning against God. Romans 5:8–9 explains that even while we were still sinners, Christ died for us. Jesus took the wrath of God which we deserved, and paid the price for our sin. Romans 6:23 promises eternal life to those who trust in Christ. Romans 10:9–10 explains that we can respond

to God's grace by confessing with our mouth that Jesus is Lord, and believing in our hearts that God raised Him from the dead.

Chapter 10
FOR GENERATIONS TO COME

1. William Bradford, *Of Plymouth Plantation* (Mineola, NY: Dover, 2006), 21.

ABOUT THE AUTHOR

ROB RIENOW'S MOST IMPORTANT ministry is loving his wife, Amy, and impressing the hearts of their six children with a love for God. He serves as the family pastor at Wheaton Bible Church in Wheaton, Illinois. He founded a ministry called Visionary Parenting, which is dedicated to equipping parents and grandparents to pass faith to their children, and to helping churches build biblical family ministries. Rob is the author of *God's Grand Vision for the Home*, *Visionary Parenting*, and *Visionary Marriage*. He holds master's degrees from Wheaton College Graduate School and Trinity International University, and a Doctor of Ministry degree from Gordon-Conwell Theological Seminary.

Would you like to share the message of this book with your friends or church family? *When They Turn Away* is available in a four-part DVD series designed for small groups or adult classes. Rob is also available to speak at conferences. Hosting a live conference is a powerful way to have an impact on your community. To get more information about the DVD series or hosting a conference, visit www.VisionaryParenting.com.

NOTES

Chapter I
HOW COULD THIS HAPPEN?

1. The Barna Group, "Most Twentysomethings Put Christianity on the Shelf Following Spiritually Active Teen Years," September 11, 2006, http://www.barna.org/barna-update/article/16 -teensnext-gen/147-most-twentysomethings-put-christianity -on-the-shelf-following-spiritually-active-teen -years.

2. Polly House, "Survey Notes Heightened Challenge of Reaching Children for Christ," *Baptist Press*, October 20, 2000, http://www.bpnews.net/bpnews.asp?id=6704.

3. See Greater Europe Mission, http://www.gemission.org/Why /statistics.asp.

4. Science textbooks in the public school system are written from the standpoint of atheistic evolution. The curriculum presupposes a materialistic and naturalistic worldview. Parents have to take school boards to court in an effort to even have "intelligent design" taught as a scientific alternative to atheistic evolution. Health classes are taught with an amoral framework. In one Illinois high school, freshmen were encouraged to question whether or not they were homosexual. The first question on the survey was, "Is it possible that if you experienced some good same-gender sex that you would discover that you were a homosexual?" Sexual discovery and experience are the highest values. Similar to the issue of creationism, if parents want abstinence taught in the public school, it often requires a court battle. To illustrate the radical changes that have taken place

in the public school system and structure, consider this quote from the National Education Association (NEA) from 1892, "If the study of the Bible is to be excluded from all state schools; if the inculcation of the principles of Christianity is to have no place in the daily program; if the worship of God is to form no part of the general exercises of these public elementary schools; then the good of the state would be better served by restoring all schools to church control." (Quoted by Os Hillman, "History of Education in America," Reclaiming the 7 Mountains of Culture, http://www.reclaim7mountains.com/apps/articles /default.asp?articleid=62624&columnid=4333.)

5. Chuck Colson, "Heather Has Two Mommies: Homosexual Agenda for Schools," Breakpoint Commentaries, September 2, 1992, http://www.breakpoint.org/commentaries/2073-heather -has-two-mommies.

6. The full text of the Presidential Proclamation, September 28, 2009, is available at http://www.whitehouse.gov/the_press_office /Presidential-Proclamation-Family-Day-2009/.

7. If you are interested in exploring this important topic further, I recommend *What If Jesus Had Never Been Born?* by D. James Kennedy and *Excused Absence: Should Christian Kids Leave Public Schools?* by Douglas Wilson.

Chapter 2
THE PERFECT STORM

1. Eric Wallace, *Uniting Church and Home* (Lorton, VA: Solutions for Integrating Church and Home, 1999), 75.

2. Tom Eldredge, *Safely Home* (San Antonio, TX: The Vision Forum, 2002), 6.

3. Christian Smith, *Soul Searching* (New York: Oxford University Press, 2005), 28.

4. The Statue of Liberty—Ellis Island Foundation, Inc., Annual Report, "Year in Review," March 31, 2008, http://www.ellisisland .org/EIinfo/Annual_Report_2008.pdf.

5. Here we find another devastating outcome in a culture that embraces the theory of atheistic evolution. As the theory of evolution takes root in the worldview of a culture, two out-

comes are assured. Both the old and the young will be increasingly marginalized and discarded. As "survival of the fittest" is carried out in reality, those who are increasingly less fit (the aged, the young, the sick, the mentally ill) are first given less respect, then fewer resources, and in officially atheistic nations such as Nazi Germany, some are eliminated.

> Forced sterilization in Germany was the forerunner of the systematic killing of the mentally ill and the handicapped. In October 1939, Hitler himself initiated a decree which empowered physicians to grant a "mercy death" to "patients considered incurable according to the best available human judgment of their state of health." The intent of the so-called "euthanasia" program, however, was not to relieve the suffering of the chronically ill. The Nazi regime used the term as a euphemism: its aim was to exterminate the mentally ill and the handicapped, thus "cleansing" the "Aryan" race of persons considered genetically defective and a financial burden to society. (Jewish Virtual Library, "Nazi Persecution of the Mentally and Physically Disabled," http://www.jewishvirtuallibrary.org/jsource/Holocaust/disabled.html)

"Survival of the fittest" is a sickening evil, an abomination to God, and outright rebellion against the fifth commandment in Exodus 20:12, "honor your father and your mother."

6. George Barna, *Transforming Children into Spiritual Champions* (Ventura, CA: Regal, 2003), 78.
7. Because of the clear teaching in Scripture that parents and grandparents are to be the primary spiritual shepherds of their children, we are working toward a model where our youth and children's ministry workers focus on equipping parents and grandparents to disciple their children at home.
8. This excerpt has been adapted from the full text of "The Directory for Family Worship," which is available at the resource library of the Free Church of Scotland Web site, http://www.freechurch.org/resources/confessions/family.htm.
9. Jonathan Edwards, "Farewell Sermon," in *The Life of President Edwards* by Sereno Edwards Dwight (New York: Carvill, 1830), 648.

10. The full text of Spurgeon's article is available at The Spurgeon Archive, maintained by Phillip R. Johnson, http://www.spurgeon .org/revival.htm.
11. Jacob Abbott, *Training Children in Godliness*, rev. and ed. by Michael J. McHugh (Arlington Heights, IL: Christian Liberty Press, 1992), 117.

Chapter 3
HOPE

1. Abraham Piper, "Prodigals—Let Them Come Home," Center for Parent/Youth Understanding, from the September 2007 issue of *Decision* magazine, http://www.cpyu.org/Page.aspx?id =365925.

Chapter 4
OFFER YOUR HEART TO THE LORD

1. While the word *generations* is not explicitly repeated in the Hebrew text, it is directly implied, and frequently included in English translations.
2. Is your family struggling with destructive generational patterns? God has the power to break those patterns and stop them from being passed to your children and grandchildren. *The Bondage Breaker* by Neil Anderson (Eugene, OR: Harvest House, 2006) will equip you with a biblical foundation for this spiritual battle.
3. Adapted from Stormie Omartian, *The Power of a Praying Parent* (Eugene, OR: Harvest House, 1995), 153–54.

Chapter 5
TURN YOUR HEART TO YOUR CHILD

1. Thank you to Richard Ross for showing this to me in the Scriptures. To find out more about his dynamic ministry of turning the hearts of parents to their children, see http://www.richardaross .com.
2. Billy Graham, *Just As I Am* (New York: HarperOne, 2007), 702, 723–24.